Instructor's M

to accompany

The Ethics
of MANAGEMENT

Fourth Edition

LaRue Tone Hosmer
Durr-Fillauer Chair in Business Ethics
University of Alabama

McGraw-Hill
Irwin

Boston   Burr Ridge, IL   Dubuque, IA   Madison, WI   New York   San Francisco   St. Louis
Bangkok   Bogotá   Caracas   Kuala Lumpur   Lisbon   London   Madrid   Mexico City
Milan   Montreal   New Delhi   Santiago   Seoul   Singapore   Sydney   Taipei   Toronto

McGraw-Hill Higher Education

A Division of The McGraw-Hill Companies

Instructor's Manual to accompany
THE ETHICS OF MANAGEMENT
LaRue Tone Hosmer

2 3 4 5 6 7 8 9 0 QSR/QSR 0 9 8 7 6 5 4 3

ISBN 0-07-304032-0

www.mhhe.com

Index

General Suggestions for Teaching the Ethics of Management

I am writing this teaching note on the assumption that the reader, doubtless a faculty member at a college or university, does not have a graduate degree in Normative Philosophy and does not have extensive experience teaching a formal course in Business Ethics or, as I prefer to term the subject area, the Ethics of Management. I prefer the latter phrase because "business ethics" to me always seems to imply that our moral standards in business differ in some way from those of our personal life; that there are a special set of ethics for use during the weekdays, and another set for use on weekends. And, of course, use of the term "business ethics" always leaves one open to the cynical but inaccurate rejoinder that "there are no ethics in business."

I don't accept either allegation. I think that we have obligations to other people within our society, and that those obligations remain the same whether we are acting as a business executive or as a private citizen. I agree that it is more difficult to fulfill those obligations in business, due to the conflicts that exist between the economic obligations to the stockholders and the social obligations to the employees, etc., but I think that our ethical beliefs and moral standards remain the same, regardless of our positions. Ethical beliefs and moral standards are not gray flannel suits that we can put on and take off to meet our differing situations. Ethical beliefs and moral standards are very basic elements in our character, and very intense influences upon our decisions and actions. The difficulty is that most business managers don't know how to apply the beliefs and standards they hold to the ethical problems they encounter. That is the reason for a course on the ethics of management.

If you do have a graduate degree in Normative Philosophy or if you have extensive experience teaching in the area of the Ethics of Management, then I am pleased that you are considering the adoption of my book. But, this teaching note is going to be too simple for you. I am writing it for the faculty member who is fully competent in his or her own field of expertise, be that Marketing Management or Operations Research or Financial Accounting, but who has had little or no experience in ethical analysis and little or no training in Normative Philosophy.

For those people, my major recommendation is, "don't worry." Ethical analysis is needed, but you have had more experience with that in your personal life than you are willing to credit to yourself. Normative Philosophy is also needed, but the concepts are basically simple. Remember that normative philosophers – i.e., those who work with *what should be*, as ethicists, rather than with *what is*, as empiricists – have been unable to reach agreement for over 2,400 years, since before the time of Socrates, so that no one can prove that you are wrong. The only thing you need in order to teach a successful module or section of a course on the ethics of management is a desire to bring business students to think in a structured, orderly way about their obligations to other people.

The purpose of a module or a section of a course on the ethics of management, then, is to bring students to think in a structured, orderly way about their obligations to other people. If you agree that the managers of business organizations (and those in non-profit institutions as well) have obligations to other members of society, but feel yourself to be somewhat inexperienced or untrained in any formal means of analysis of those obligations, then I have some suggestions on the design of the course section or module you are to offer. You are welcome, obviously, to agree or disagree here. What I would like to do is to explain what seemed to work well at Michigan, when I offered a 14 session module on ethics at that university, and to provide a brief synopsis of the structure and content that can be used in a submission to a Curriculum Committee, if that is required at your college or university. This is a personal account, but let me explain that I am now retired at Michigan, but was then offered and have since accepted an endowed chair here at Alabama. I still teach the ethics of management, but now in a 28-session class. I don't use the *Ethics of Management* 4th Edition in this longer class, but I do use all of the materials from that edition.

My belief is that a module on the ethics of management 1) should be short, between 7 and 14 class sessions; 2) should be direct, with a few very clearly stated objectives; 3) should be focused, on three very basic concepts; 4) should move along quickly, to maintain the interest of the students; and 5) should attempt to convey a method of analysis, not a standard of behavior. Let me take up each one of these recommendations, in sequence:

1. Should be short. The book, *Ethics of Management*, is designed to be used as a supplemental text in an existing course in Business Policy, Business and Society, Business Law, or any of the functional and technical specialties taught at business schools. It is also designed, and this is the way in which I used the book, to be the major text in a 14 class session, 1-1/2 credit hour course focusing specifically on ethical problems and ethical analysis. Whichever form you adopt, let me suggest that you plan on spending ten (at the fewest) to fourteen (for the module) class sessions on those topics. There are three basic reasons for this:

    Doubtful students. Ethical problems and ethical analysis are important in business management, and I agree that those topics should not be short-changed in management education. Yet, you will find that most students enter the course with a questioning attitude; most of the other courses they have taken in management have emphasized that their sole responsibilities are to maximize profits within the constraints of the law. I think that you want to deal directly with those issues, and do that quickly, forcefully and briefly.

    Imprecise methods. In every other course that students take, particularly in the first year of either a BBA or MBA program, they find very precise rules to be followed. Debits always go on the left. Investors always select projects with the highest risk-adjusted rates of return. Marketing programs always integrate price, distribution and promotion to match product characteristics and market positions. There are no equivalent rules to be followed in the formulation of ethical decisions. Again, be quick, forceful and brief.

    Involved discussions. Therefore I suggest a ten to fourteen session course. I think that it is important to say, in essence, "Here are current examples of ethical problems" and "Here are alternative means of analyzing those problems" and then let them analyze those problems, using those methods, so they become comfortable and confident that they can form their own judgments. I think that in ten to fourteen involved, active class sessions students will become comfortable and confident in expressing their personal judgments.

2. <u>Should be direct</u>. I think that it is also important in a module on the ethics of management not to try to do too much. You cannot provide students with firm rules for the resolution of every type of ethical dilemma. You cannot show students, even if you wished to, how to lead lives of ethical purity. You cannot discuss with students every major problem within our society. What you can do is to help them to recognize ethical dilemmas when they appear, provide them with alternative means of resolving those dilemmas, and offer them the self-confidence to choose among those means. Those are the objectives I set for the course:

Recognition of ethical problems. Obligations to others are at the heart of the ethics of management. Managers are people who decide, and those decisions can affect other people both positively and negatively. The basic argument of a course of managerial ethics is that this impact upon others must always be included in the decision process. The first objective of the course, then, is to get students to recognize these impacts, particularly the negative ones that can cause hurt or harm to others, or interfere with their rights.

Understanding of ethical analysis. In most managerial decisions, the positive results outweigh the negative impacts. In some, however, the hurts or harms outweigh the benefits. The function of ethical analysis is to find a balance that is "right" and "just" and "fair". This balance can be found by thinking through the economic, legal and ethical consequences of a managerial decision in a logical, structured way. The second goal of the course, then, is to introduce students to this logical, structured analytical process.

Reliance upon personal values. The analysis of an ethical problem may be objective, following a logical and structured process, but the final choice depends upon a subjective scale – the norms, beliefs and values of the individual making the decision. There is no agreement among normative philosophers or management faculty upon an objective scale for ethical choice. Consequently, the third goal of the course is to assist students in examining their norms, beliefs and values, and thus gaining the self-confidence necessary to rely upon those norms, beliefs and values in making firm ethical decisions.

3. <u>Should be focused</u>. Now that I have expressed my personal recommendations on the abbreviated length and limited objectives of a module on the ethics of management – recommendations with which, again, you are free to disagree – let me go on and explain my personal suggestions on the content. I think that the course should be dominated by three beliefs:

Ethical problems in management are pervasive. Ethical problems go far beyond the simple issues of collusion, theft and bribery, and extend into all of the functional and technical areas of business. Why? Business managers make decisions and take actions that affect other people. If those decisions and actions affect other people adversely, if they hurt or harm those people in ways beyond their individual control, then we have an ethical problem that requires some analysis of the social consequences, in addition to the more common analysis of the financial results and legal rules.

Ethical problems in management are complex. Ethical problems, again, go far beyond the simple "yes, I will" or "no, I won't" choices between immediate financial benefits and obvious social costs, where all that is needed is a very elementary level of ethical consciousness to compare the two and make the decision. Instead there are extended consequences, multiple alternatives, mixed outcomes, uncertain occurrences and personal implications that complicate the analysis of the financial, legal and social consequences in ethical problems.

Ethical standards in management are personal. There is no single, fundamental rule that can be applied to all ethical problems in all situations, and consequently there is no way I can prove that my standards for choice are, in some way, better than those of the students'. Therefore, there can be no lecturing in the class on the "right" way to decide. What there can be is discussion of alternative "right" ways to act, based upon personal moral standards of behavior that have been examined according to basic ethical principles or underlying ethical values.

4. <u>Should be lively</u>. This is essentially a repetition of my first comment above, on the suggested length of the course, but I think that it is critical to the success of a course on the ethics of management so let me repeat my concerns. Students at the University of Michigan, particularly in the undergraduate sections, approached ethics with an unfortunate degree of wariness and suspicion, not with a burst of enthusiasm. It was hard to get class discussion going; no one wanted to be the first to express a "do good" or "be good" sentiment and appear to be personally naïve or socially concerned before his or her peers. The same hesitancy is present at the University of Alabama, though to a somewhat lesser extent. I hope that it is different at your college or university, but I assume that it is not. Consequently I have some very explicit suggestions on ways to increase student interest and decrease student hesitancy. I will discuss these methods in the sections that follow on the use of descriptive films and videos, in-class discussion groups, a demanding syllabus, and an aggressive first class meeting. But first, let me emphasize once again the need to provide students with a method of analysis they can use to resolve ethical issues.

5. <u>Should focus on a method of analysis, not a standard of behavior.</u> This is the recommendation that I want to convey as strongly as I possibly can. Provide your students with a solid analytical methodology which they can first use to determine what is "right", "just" and "fair" in their own minds, and which they can then use to convince others. If you do that, and add interesting films and videos, in-class discussion groups, a demanding syllabus and a forceful first class, I think you will have a successful course. Here, in summary, is the method of analysis I suggest:

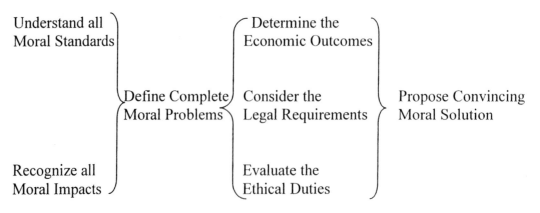

Understand all Moral Standards — Recognize all Moral Impacts → Define Complete Moral Problems → Determine the Economic Outcomes, Consider the Legal Requirements, Evaluate the Ethical Duties → Propose Convincing Moral Solution

Interesting Films and Videos

I use a lot of films and videos in the classroom. Students like them, of course, but I don't use them to cater to students likes or dislikes. I find that discussions start much more naturally after students have watched a film or videotape that visually depicts a moral problem, where they are forced to watch and listen to the people impacted by that problem. The visible and audible aspects of film and video are, for ethical problems, a great improvement over the more sterile nature of written cases in which the people involved necessarily remain abstractions. Students, similar to all the rest of us, feel much more sympathetic to people they know, and films and videos provide the necessary introduction.

The problem is that there are not that many really good films and videotapes available. My definition of a "really good" film or videotape is one that is short (about 15 minutes, so there is plenty of time left for discussion), realistic (portrays a situation that the students do not feel is contrived), and may or may not be related to business (students are more willing to discuss moral problems that are outside their profession; moral problems in law or medicine tend to spark greater interest than those in management). Here are the films and videos that I recommend; I generally show only a very short section from the films:

1. *Wall Street* and the "greed is good" speech. This film is readily available on tape from any rental store. The speech, about 5 minutes long, comes 2/3rds of the way through the film, at a meeting of the stockholders of the paper company that the villain, Gordon Gheko, plans to acquire in a hostile takeover. The scene and staging are very well done. The speech is short and to the point. It provides a great start to the class discussion. I explain that this is the speech that Ivan Boesky (all this is far enough in the past that I have to explain to the students who Ivan Boesky was) gave to MBA students at the University of California at Berkeley, and they stood up and cheered. Then I ask, "Would you stand up and cheer? Is greed really that good"? The responses I get are described in the teaching note for Chapter II on "Moral Analysis and Economic Outcomes".

2. *The Big One* and the interview with Philip Knight, founder and chairman of Nike. This film was produced by Michael Moore, who also made the much better known *Roger and Me*, about his effort to find Roger Smith, Chairman of General Motors, to talk about plant closings. That film was one-sided and opinionated, but it was amusing. This film is equally one-sided, but far less amusing. However, there is one good section: the interview with Philip Knight, chairman of Nike, the athletic shoe manufacturer and marketer, who attempts to avoid accepting responsibility for workplace conditions in 3rd world countries. Michael Moore invites the chairman to go with him to Indonesia to visit the shoe factories in that country, but is rebuffed. That provides a good start to the class discussion, "Why doesn't Philip Knight want to go to see the conditions at factories that produce shoes for Nike? Again, the responses I get are described in the teaching note for Chapter I on "Moral Problems in Business Management.

3. *Erin Brockovich* and the meeting of Erin with the condescending attorneys from the much larger law firm, in which she presents them with the material that she has gathered that will enable them to win or settle the case, and then her meeting with a client whose health has

been very adversely affected in which she tells that person about the settlement. This is a reasonably recent film, and most of my students have seen it. The issue, as you doubtless know, is the alleged pollution of ground water with chromium near a natural gas pumping station owned by the Pacific Gas and Electric Company in Hinkley, California, a high desert community where the ground water was used for the municipal water supply. Chromium had been added to the water used for cooling at the pumping station to prevent rusting of the piping in that cooling system. The problem was that this water had been stored in unlined lagoons. Chromium is a heavy metal that – it was alleged, though this is still in dispute – has severe health effects. The film is very current in the life style portrayed, which adds to the interest, and identifies the company and other participants by name, which adds to the believability, but there are not many sections that summarize the issues. I use the 5 minute section that I described above; it occurs near the end. The film is, of course, readily available from video rental stores

4. *A Question of Power: HydroQuebec and the Great Whale Generating Project* (33 minutes). This is the first of three videos that we produced at the University of Michigan while I was on the faculty at that institution. It visually depicts the decision faced by HydroQuebec, a large public utility owned by the province of Quebec, whether or not to build a huge hydroelectric generating station in the remote wilderness of northern Canada. This situation is described under the subheading "Example of a Large Scale Moral Problem" at the start of Chapter I on "The Nature of Moral Problems". I sometimes use this video for the discussion in the 2nd class, after the students have read that introductory chapter, but more frequently in the 10th class, as a way of pulling together the economic, legal and ethical forms of analysis before we move on to organizational, rather than moral, issues. My teaching notes are included in the discussions of cases following Chapter IV.

5. *Your Job or Mine: Green Giants Decision to Move to Mexico* (23 minutes). This is the second of the three videos that we produced at the University of Michigan while I was there. It visually depicts the decision made by Green Giant Corp., the producer of frozen food products, to move from Salinas in northern California to Irapuato in central Mexico, with a very large saving in labor costs though at considerable social cost to Salinas and environmental cost to Irapuato. This situation is described in the case "Green Giant and the Move to Mexico" that follows Chapter II. I use it either to start the discussion at the beginning of the class after it has been assigned, or at the end of the previous class to improve the interest in preparing for that discussion. My teaching notes are included in the discussions of cases following Chapter II.

The University of Michigan no longer has a system in place to handle the distribution of these videos (and a third one, *Violence on Television*). Consequently, if you call me (205) 358-8931 or use e-mail (Lhosmer@cba.ua.edu) at the University of Alabama, I will arrange to have a videocassette with all three sent to you at no charge.

In-Class Discussion Groups

My classes usually contain 50 to 60 students. It is often difficult, as I have mentioned previously, to get meaningful class discussions started in that large a section. Students are hesitant to get involved, and the reason – in my view – is that they have been told so many times, particularly in the introductory courses on economics and accounting, that the sole responsibility of managers is to maximize stockholder value within the constraints of the law that they are slow to express contrary views. They apparently don't, as I mentioned before, want to express their social concerns in the very public forum that is a classroom with 50 to 60 friends and peers.. Consequently I frequently break up the full class into either "small" or "large" discussion groups.

The small discussion groups consist of students who sit close to each other and, I assume, know each other. I take a seating chart and mark, with clear borders, blocks of three to four students who sit in near proximity to each other, and identify each of those groups with a number or letter. I display that seating chart on the vue-graph or – my preference – hand out copies of that marked-up seating chart. I prefer handing out copies because then members of each group have a record of the names of the other members. I then give those groups 15 minutes to determine what the management in a previously assigned and prepared case should do, and why. Each group is to write their recommendation and rationale on a vue graph slide, and be ready to present it to the class. I provide blank vue-graph slides, together with felt tipped pens for writing and paper towels for clean-up. Vue graph or transparency slides that can be used only for writing, but not for printing from a prepared document in a copy machine, are available from office supply stores at sharply reduced prices.

After 15 minutes I call upon the members of one of those small groups to come down and make their presentation to the balance of the class. After the first presentation, which is usually followed at the start of the term by only desultory questions or comments, I ask for a group that disagrees. Usually there is at least one, and that 2nd presentation will make the differences apparent, and get the discussion going. If not, then I summarize the differences on the board, and call upon students to explain which side they are on, and why. I continually emphasize the "and why" rationale because, of course, that is what this series of classes on the ethics of management is all about. I find that once I get students talking about their reasons, which are defendable, rather than their opinions, which are not, the reluctance to participate in class discussions goes away.

The large discussion groups consist of 6 to 8 students who are selected at random from the class list. I select names from the class list the day before to form the groups, and then print out a "group assignment" sheet with an identifying letter or number for each of those groups. I make copies of that sheet and then distribute those copies at the start of class. One of the members of each groups is identified as the "leader" for that day, generally by marking his/her name with an asterisk. The leader is responsible for organizing the discussion, making certain that each member has an opportunity to express his/her opinion, taking a vote, and then preparing the report. In the event that the members of the group do not agree on a single recommendation, they are permitted to break up into subgroups, and prepare different reports. I give these large groups 20 minutes to reach a decision, and tell them that they are free to leave the room. Most do. At the start I used to worry that some of the groups would go down to the coffee shop and talk about other social or athletic matters, but that does not seem to happen. I get some very solidly prepared reports.

Many of the students in my classes do not know one another, so I find it is necessary at the start of the term to put post-it notes on the wall with identifying numbers or letters so that the members of each group can find each other easily. After the groups reassemble in 20 minutes – another of the duties of the group leader is to get the members back on time – I call upon groups to make presentations and – as with the smaller in-class discussion groups – their presentations make the differences clear. I strongly suggest that you try both the small "in-class" and large "break out" discussion groups; they seem to make members of my classes feel much more comfortable about expressing their recommendations and reasons on controversial issues.

Demanding Syllabus

Given the suggested classroom use of interesting films and videos, the advised division of the class into small and large discussion groups, the recommended focus on the recognition and resolution of moral problems, and the proposed employment of economic, legal and ethics means of analysis of those problems, how do I fit all this together? The following is my suggested schedule for a 14 class module or course section. I pack in lots of material: ·

Class 1   No assignment. I think that most of us use the first class meeting to describe the intellectual content and grading standards of the course. It is important, however, that the students not see this first class as an easy "throw-away" session
- I focus on the intellectual content, and use the five vue-graph slides that are part of this Teacher's Guide, printed directly following directly behind this "Demanding Syllabus" section.
- I also use one of the very short videos described in an earlier part of this "Suggestions" part of the Teacher's Guide. The one that seems to work best is from Michael Moore's *The Big One* on producing athletic shoes abroad.

Class 2   Read Chapter I on "Moral Problems in Management" and prepare two cases: "Cruise Ships and the Disposal of Waste at Sea" and "Napster and the Free Exchange of Recorded Music"
- I assign the first case to the front half of the room and the second case to the back half. I then divide each half into groups of four to five students; those groups are to meet for 20 minutes, and decide if the action is "right".
- I like small group discussions because they break up the class and get everyone involved. The groups are to cite reasons from economics, law and ethics supporting their opinion, and write a report to the class on a vue-graph slide.

Class 3   Prepare "Whirlpool Corporation and the Sale of Dish Antennas". I use the case as the basis for a full class discussion, and then the balance of the class time to review the content of Chapter I.

Class 4   Read Chapter II on "Moral Analysis and Economic Outcomes" and prepare either "Susan Shapiro and the Extent of Workplace Safety" and/or "World Bank and the Export of Pollution".

- I use the "Greed is Good" speech from the motion picture *Wall Street* at the start. It is only two minutes long, but it gets across very clearly, despite being delivered by the villain of the film, the moral content of economic theory.
- My recommendation is that you use the "Susan Shapiro" case; this is much more business policy oriented than the World Bank one, which is focused on public policy. Both seem to generate student interest, however.

Class 5   Prepare "Green Giant and the Move to Mexico". There is a 20 minute video that shows the people described in this case. I generally show the video at the end pf the previous class, and then for this class use the large "break-out" discussion groups.

Class 6   Read Chapter III on "Moral Analysis and Legal Requirements" and prepare "Sarah Goodwin and the Extent of Consumer Protection" and/or "Johnson Controls and the Place of Gender Equality"
- I assign the first case to the front half of the room and the second case to the back half. As before, I divide each half into groups of four to five students; those groups are to meet for 20 minutes, and decide what they would do.

Class 7   Prepare H. B. Fuller and the Sale of Resistol. This is a great case, written by Norman Bowie and Stephanie Lenway, both of the Carlson School of Management at the University of Minnesota.
- I often divide the class into 8 to 10 person Boards of Directors for H. B. Fuller Company; they are told to meet for 20 minutes, and come up with a recommendation to continue or to stop the sale of Resistol.

Class 8   Read Chapter IV on "Moral Analysis and Ethical Duties". Students have generally had an introductory course on Economics so they understand the basics there, and they've seen enough courtroom dramas on television and film so the processes of the law are reasonably familiar, but the principles of normative ethics are totally foreign to them.
- Consequently, I just assign this chapter by itself, without any cases. Then, I start the class by distributing one or two of the short cases, termed "starters", that are printed in the last section of this Introduction
- Or, you can use the two cases: "The Good Life at RJR Nabisco and "The Leveraged Buyout of RJR Nabisco. In both the actions of management are fully legal, and in "Leveraged Buyout" they are economically efficient.

Class 9   Prepare "WalMart Stores in Northern Michigan" This is another of the good summary cases. The proposed action by WalMart is economically efficient and borderline lawful, but there is no questions but that a large number of people are going to be harmed and/or have their rights infringed.
- I often divide the class here into 8 to 10 person Boards of Directors for WalMart; they are told to meet for 20 minutes, and come up with a recommendation to build or not build the large store and mall in Petoskey.

Class 10   Review Chapter II On "Economic Outcomes", Chapter III on "Legal Requirements" and Chapter IV on "Ethical Duties". I try to use this class, 2/3rds of the way through the module, to pull the analytical parts of the course together.

- I show the video on "HydroQuebec and the Great Whale Project" described in the earlier portion of this Introduction, and then work through the analytical process in detail. Students realize they do feel comfortable with this process.

Class 11   Read Chapter V on "Why Should a Business Manager Be Moral?" and prepare all three short cases on "Johnson and Johnson and the Recall of Tylenol", "Herman Miller and the Protection of the Environment" and "Merck Corporation and the Cure for River Blindness".

- I divide the class into thirds (right, center and left) , and assign each of the cases to one of those sections. Then at the start of class I have groups within each section decide what should be done, and put their reasons on vue-graph.
- The conceptual content of this part of the course is reasonably simple and direct: to succeed in a competitive business it is necessary to build trust, commitment and effort, and to get trust it is necessary to treat stakeholders fairly

Class 12   Reach Chapter VI on "How Can a Business Organization Be Made Moral?" Here the course comes back to Values, Goals, Mission Statements, Financial Supports, Performance Measures, etc. Students are generally familiar with these concepts

- I show a 5 minute portion of the film *Erin Brockovich*. The portion I select is where Erin has found the incriminating documents that force PG&E to settle. Almost all students have seen this film; it provides another familiar aspect.
- The question for class discussion is, "Assuming that the film is correct in its allegations about the harmful aspects of chromium in drinking water, how could PG&E have avoided this $330 million penalty and disastrous pr hit?

Class 13   Prepare "Two Companies in Need of Redirection". The chemical company that hired Susan Shapiro and the department store that hired Sarah Goodwin both were assessed very severe penalties, and the senior executives at both were fired, as a result of the actions described in the cases

- Again, I generally assign the first case to the front half of the room, and the second case to the back half. Then, during the class, I break those sections into groups, with each group to prepare a report for the balance of the class.
- Here I do things differently, however. I have one group develop a mission statement for "their" company. Another is to prepare a list of performance measures and incentive payments. A third a list of prohibited actions. etc..

Class 14   Prepare "McKinsley Advertising Company". I use this case as a summary for the course. By this time members of the class know each other so I ask them to form groups of three to four students. Then I divide those groups into fourths, with a specific assignment for each third:

- Groups in the 1st quarter are to decide if the action – promoting the use of a new type of radar speed detector – is "right" or "wrong", and to prepare a report on vue-graph slides or Power Point.

- Groups in the 2nd quarter are to assume that the senior executives have decided that promoting speed detectors is "right" and they prepare a report on values, goals, a mission statement, etc. based upon that assumption.
- Groups in the 3rd quarter are to assume that the senior executive have decided that promoting speed detectors is "wrong" and they are to state values and goals, prepare a mission statement, etc. based upon that assumption.
- Groups in the 4th quarter are to make their own decision as to the proposed action is "right" or "wrong", but they are to show why that position and the supporting values, etc. will lead towards trust, commitment and effort
- Instead of giving the groups time during the class to prepare their reports, I generally insist that the groups meet prior to class and come in with their reports prepared and ready for presentation. It is a good way to end the course.

Aggressive First Class

"Aggressive" is not a good choice of words, but I can't think of another that equally conveys my intent. I think that it is important that the first class not be viewed as a "throw-away session by the students for that relaxed "this is not important" attitude will carry over into subsequent sessions. On the first day I try to solidly get across the feeling 1) that there is a lot of material to be covered; 2) that this material is important to the practice of management; 3) that it is necessary to get started quickly in order to cover this important material thoroughly; and 4) that this important material which is to be covered thoroughly is going to be a heck of a lot more interesting than they (the students) had expected. Let me repeat again: many of your students are going to come to the first class with the expectation that this course section or module is going to focus on such simple moral standards as "Don't lie, cheat or steal" which they feel they already know, or on such elementary moral injunctions as "Always treat other people well, and never harm the environment" which they believe cannot always be followed. I would suggest strongly that you disabuse them of those preconceptions, and use the slides (given on the last five pages) to summarize the intellectual content of the course forthrightly and exactly.

Conclusions

My most important recommendation is that you teach methods of analysis, not standards of behavior. You will often hear it stated that students, by the time that they have reached the junior or senior years at an undergraduate college, or the 1st or 2nd years of a graduate program, have moral standards that are set by their parents, their churches, their schools and their associates, and that consequently you can't teach moral standards of behavior. I agree wholeheartedly, but I also belief that changing moral standards of behavior is far less important than learning to recognize and resolve moral problems through the rigorous application of solid conceptual frameworks drawn from economics, law and ethics to arrive at convincing moral solutions. Those methods of analysis are expressed in the five graphics that are reproduced on the following pages in type large enough to be put onto vuegraph slides.

Complex Nature of Moral Problems in Business

Benefits for Some

Harms to Others   Moral Problems
                            in a

Rights Exercised   Business Firm

Rights Denied

Derivation of Subjective Standards of Moral Behavior

Religious/Cultural
Traditions

↓

Personal Goals
Personal Norms   Subjective Standards
Personal Beliefs   of Moral Behavior
Personal Values

↑

Economic/Social
Situations

Application of Objective Methods of Moral Analysis

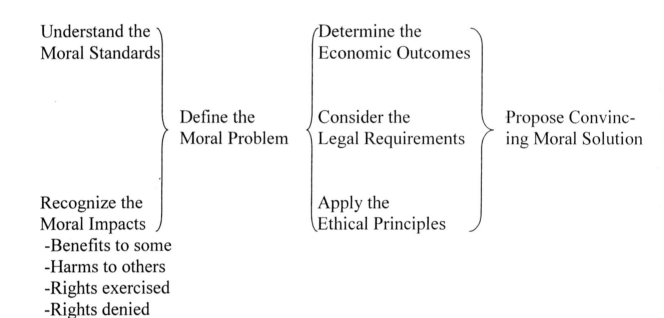

Understand the
Moral Standards

Recognize the
Moral Impacts
 -Benefits to some
 -Harms to others
 -Rights exercised
 -Rights denied

Define the
Moral Problem

Determine the
Economic Outcomes

Consider the
Legal Requirements

Apply the
Ethical Principles

Propose Convinc-
ing Moral Solution

Building Trust, Commitment and Effort within an Organization

Corporate Mgt.
in Extended
Organizations

Recognition of Moral
Problems
-   What is "duty"?

Application of Moral
Reasoning
-What is "right"?

Possession of Moral
Character
-What is "integrity"?

Trust
Commitment
Effort

Extending Cooperation, Innovation and Unification

Managerial
balancing:
-Economic benefits
-Legal requirements
-Ethical Principles

{
Organizational
Values

Corporate
Goals

Mission
Statement

Financial
Supports

Performance
Measures

Incentive
Payments

Prohibited
Procedures

Leadership
Actions
}

Trust
Commitment ⟶ Innovation
Effort

Cooperation
Innovation
Unification

Teaching Notes for Chapter I – Moral Problems in Business Management

The basic argument in this chapter is that moral problems are not moral because a respected moral authority says that they are. They are moral because some people are hurt or harmed in ways outside their own control, or have their rights ignored, while others are benefited or helped, and have their rights respected. It is this conflict between benefits and harms, between rights respected and rights ignored, that generates the special conditions of a moral problem. And, it is this conflict between benefits and harms, between rights and wrongs, that makes these moral problems so difficult to resolve. How do you decide if the benefits to some are large enough to overcome the harms to others, or if the rights of some are important enough to deny the rights of others. The process for solution proposed by this text was summarized in a graphic that was provided at both the start and the conclusion of Chapter I. It is repeated below for emphasis:

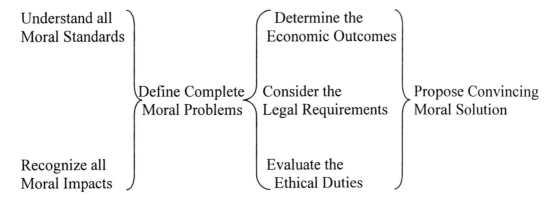

For the first three to four class sessions I draw out this graphic on the board, so that it is clear, and then I use that graphic to guide, not to force, the class discussion of the cases. I also draw out on the board the other graphic that was printed in Chapter I, on the determination of individual moral standards. I want to continually emphasize, during the discussion of the cases, that we do differ in our moral outlooks for perfectly legitimate reasons:

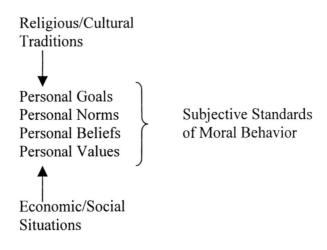

This, and the other teaching notes on the chapters in the text, will follow the same format with 1) assignment questions, 2) start-up methods, 3) discussion issues, and 4) an analytical outline for each of the three cases:

1. Assignment questions. I do not use assignment questions because I find that they are generally ignored in the students' preparation. You may have better luck that I with those questions, so here are some that I think would focus attention on the major issues:

What does "right" really mean? How do you know when something is truly "right" or truly "wrong?"

Why do people's views on what is "right" and "wrong" differ? Why would an unemployed sawmill worker in northern California feel differently about cutting old growth forests than a young lawyer, working in San Francisco, who enjoys hiking in the Sierras?

How do you attempt to convince people who disagree with you about what is "right" What arguments should that unemployed sawmill worker make if he/she were at a meeting with the young lawyer. What arguments should the lawyer make?

2. Start-up methods. I also do not go over the material in the text during the class, except in the form of a short "mini-lecture" at the end, because I find that class repetition generally detracts from student preparation. "Why read this material carefully tonight if we're going to talk about it throughout the class tomorrow?" seems to be the prevalent attitude. Instead, I move directly onto the discussion of the cases.

An alternative is to start the discussion by bringing into class an ethical issue that is currently in the news. Now, I realize that any example I mention in this teaching note will soon appear dated, but in the fall of 2001 a good example of a moral issues was the failure of the Firestone tires on the Ford SUVs. *Sixty Minutes* produced a video program on the early failure of those tires, in Venezuela, that is excellent, but, as described in the "Suggestions" portion of this teaching note that deals with videos, it is difficult to get copies of those programs from *Sixty Minutes*.

The topic of tire failure, however, is valid even if you use a newspaper clipping for the introduction rather than a video program. Almost all of the students have heard of the problem, and some will say that their parents had to change the Firestone tires on their family cars. The discussion of moral problems that are current enough to have affected students and/or their families forcefully conveys the idea that Business Ethics is not an obsolete and arcane subject, but one that should be important to all managers because it affects the lives and the well being of other people. The concept of "stakeholders" makes a great deal more sense if students can envisage themselves as being one of those holders.

3. Discussion issues. As explained previously, I generally do not start the early classes in the course by talking about assignment questions, or by bringing up current topics. Instead, I go directly to the cases, but with a difference. Firstly I call upon two to three students to "set the

stage" (that is describe the situation) for each of the cases. As explained in the "Suggestions" portion of this teaching note in the section dealing with the Syllabus I frequently assign two short cases rather than one, but divide up responsibility for those cases between the front and the back of the classroom. I like to pack lots of material into the class time, and provide plenty of opportunities for small group meetings. Before breaking up into those small groups I ask individual students whom I call upon at random, to describe the situation described in the case, and to list the persons who will be benefited and harmed, and those who will have their rights recognized or denied. I find that it is necessary to call upon students at the start of each class to ensure adequate preparation.

Then I divide the class into groups by passing out (or putting on the vuegraph) a copy of the class list with a group number or identifying letter after each name. At the start of the term, when students don't seem to know each other well, if at all, I also put up "post-it" notes at different places in the classroom with the group number or letter to establish a place for the group members to meet. Each group is asked to pick up a vue-graph transparency slide, a felt-tipped pen and some paper towels for corrections, told to take 20 minutes, and then come back at a set time (the set time is important; some of the groups get interested enough in what they are doing that otherwise they will come back much too late) with a report to the class on what they believe the company should do.

These "break out" groups seem to work very well. They give each member of the class an opportunity to express his or her opinion under conditions that are less imposing for many than having to speak in front of the full class, and of course they break up the time and provide an opportunity to meet other students and listen to other opinions. I used to worry that the use of these groups might be subject to abuse, and that some of the students would head for the coffee shop and spend their time talking about other issues, but that does not seem to happen frequently if at all. The groups generally come back with vue-graph slides thoughtfully prepared. When the class reassembles, after 20 minutes, I call upon one of the groups at random to come down and present their recommendation and their supporting rationale. After one group presents, of course, it is easy to ask if everyone agrees, and the protective aspects of group membership seems to make it far easier to find students willing to ask probing questions or express dissenting views. Those students are then asked to bring their group members down to the front of the room, and present their recommendation and their rationale.

I generally try to save ten minutes at the end of each class session to present a summary, usually based upon a vue-graph slide of one of the graphics from the text. These graphics has been reproduced in large type on 8-1/2" x 11" pages in the "Suggestions" part of this teacher's guide. You can use those pages to make the vue-graph slides.

The theme of these last ten minute mini-lectures is "This is what I hope you learned from this class". At the end I try to relate that learning to the next assignment, saying "Look at this next case or next chapter from this point of view", and quit. I always try to quit 5 minutes early, partially to give me time to prepare for the next class but primarily to give students an opportunity to think about the issues that have been raised. Probably most of them do not use that time to think about those issues, but some do and that – in my view – makes it worthwhile. Now, on to the cases:

Cruise Ships and the Disposal of Waste at Sea

The issue in this case is the present practice of the cruise ship lines, which primarily operate out of Miami or Fort Lauderdale in Florida and travel throughout the Caribbean, to discharge waste water overboard rather than carry it back to the home port for treatment. These are the so-called "gray water" wastes from the laundry, kitchen and showers and it all seems relatively harmless, but people who know the situation describe it as "an unsavory, smelly mess that is discharged at night in order not to concern or disturb the guests". The problem is said to be that the nutrients from the kitchen residues and the chemicals from the laundry detergents and bathroom soaps greatly increase the growth of viral and bacterial agents throughout the Caribbean, affecting the sea life of the region and decreasing the clarity of the ocean. Many of the island nations have objected, and have passed laws against the dumping, but they do not have the power to enforce their laws. I usually don't, as explained above, go through each of the steps in the moral reasoning process as described in the Chapter I graphic. Instead, I ask the "who is benefited and who is harmed" questions to ensure preparation and make certain that everyone understands the issues, and then have the students discuss those issues in small groups, but I will structure this teaching note about the questions that are derived from that graphic:

1. What groups will be benefited from continuing the present "dump at sea" policy?

> Owners and managers of the cruise lines, from higher profits
> Customers of the cruise lines, from lower prices
> Shop keepers in island nations, from undiminished numbers of customers

2. What groups will be harmed from continuing the present "dump at sea" policy?

> Residents of the island nations, from gradual deterioration of sea water
> Fisherman in the island nations, from gradual decline in quality/quantity of catch
> Everyone associated with cruise ships, if environment substantially deteriorates

3. Whose rights will be exercised by continuing the present "dump at sea" policy?

> Owners and managers who have a legal right to dump outside 3 mile limit, a maritime regulation that was set in the early 1800s when 3 miles was the range of artillery fire from a coastal battery, and consequently the limit of ability for a non-naval power to enforce national sovereignty.

4. Whose rights will be ignored by continuing the present "dump at sea" policy?

> Governments of island nations, who can't enforce their anti-dumping laws in a world court due to what they consider to be obsolete maritime regulations.

Residents of island nations, who can't control their own environment.

5. Express the moral problem so that everyone will believe that their moral concerns have been recognized and included.

    Is it right that the vacation cruise lines continue to dump gray water wastes at sea, given that 1) it financially benefits company stockholders, cruise line passengers and island nation shopkeepers, but environmentally harms residents and fishermen in the island nations; and 2) given that it is currently permissible under maritime law, but not permissible under the law of the island nations.

6. What are the economic benefits?

    There is no question but that the dumping of gray water wastes at sea meets the primary condition of economic efficiency for this creates the greatest profits for the company and the lowest prices for the consumer. It would also appear that the markets for cruise line vacations are competitive, but the counter argument would be that the customers are not fully informed given the practice of dumping a night. Lastly, and most importantly, there are external costs imposed upon the residents and fishermen of the island nations through the practice of dumping.

7. What are the legal requirements?

    World maritime laws permit the dumping of gray water wastes by the cruise ships; island nation laws prohibit the practice. The question then is which law should take precedence? The " social contract" or "veil of ignorance" answer is to try to envisage what people who did not know whether they were island nation residents or cruise line passengers and/or owners/managers would decide?

8. What are the ethical duties?

    Personal virtues. Can the managers of the cruise lines be open, honest, truthful and proud of nightly dumping at sea? The late night timing seems to belie that pride.

    Religious injunctions. Is the dumping at sea kind and compassionate? Does it create a sense of community, with everyone striving for a common goal?

    Utilitarian benefits. Does the dumping at sea create greater goods than harms for all of society. It is easy to measure the benefits; it is difficult to measure the harms.

    Universal duties. Would the owners and managers of the cruise lines, given that they had vacation homes along the coast, want other nations to dump wastes off shore?

    Distributive justice. Does the practice of dumping at sea harm the least among us, those with least income, education or power? Perhaps these are the island residents.

Contributive liberty. Does the practice of dumping at sea prevent anyone from developing their skills to the fullest? Perhaps these are the island fishermen

What is my conclusion. I tell students in my classes that I am willing to express my opinion when asked, and occasionally when I'm not asked, but that I don't want that opinion to be accepted as the only possible view. I don't think that the purpose of the course is for me to impose my norms, beliefs and values upon others. I think that the purpose of the course is to get others to think about their norms, beliefs and values.

Having said all that, in my view the dumping clearly imposes external costs upon the residents and fishermen of the island nations, and there are obvious conflicts between the maritime law of prosperous nations (those with citizens who can afford to take vacation cruises) and the environmental law of the island nations. Further, I explain, the lack of openness, the absence of common goals, and the inapplicability of universal duties all seem to indicate that the cruise lines should install holding tanks for the gray water wastes, and charge the costs of using those tanks to their customers.

Let me make one recommendation very strongly. It is necessary to get closure to all case discussions, but I would suggest that you not impose that closure by expressing your opinion alone. I think that the best way to end the class discussion of a moral problem, such as the dumping of gray water wastes in the Caribbean, is to take a vote. A vote of classmates will not make students who disagree feel that a decision has been forced upon them. Instead they will feel that they did not explain themselves well enough, or that you did not give them an opportunity to explain themselves well enough, or that – just maybe – they were wrong. Votes in my class on the need to stop discharging gray water wastes and start using shipboard holding tanks average about 80/20 in favor of those tanks.

Napster and the Free Exchange of Recorded Music

This is an interesting case to discuss because a large majority of the students have used the Napster service, and many – but certainly not all -- feel a little bit guilty about having done so. At some point this case will become dated, but that has not yet happened in my classes, probably because there are now so many new substitutes for Napster that the free exchange of recorded music continues unabated.

Once again, I usually break the class up into small discussion groups (about 4 students per group), and give those groups 20 minutes to decide whether the service is "right" or "wrong" and to prepare a vue-graph transparency that states their conclusion and their supporting rationale. Before the class breaks into those groups, however, I call upon a few students to "set the stage" and demonstrate that they are adequately prepared by describing who has been benefited, and who harmed, and whose rights have been exercised and whose rights have been denied, by the use of the Napster service. I use only the first few questions from the following listing in the class, but provide them all here as a way to structure this teaching note:

1. What groups have been benefited from the "free exchange" policy?

Younger customers, mostly students in high school and college, get music for free
Some musicians have gained wider recognition and approval through Napster
Older customers have not benefited; no one copies Beethoven's 9th over the web

2. What groups have been harmed by the "free exchange" policy?

Most artists and musicians believe that they receive lower royalties
Recording company owners and managers say they have lower profits
One of the problems here is that neither the musicians nor the executives generate much sympathy among the students; royalties and profits are believed to be huge. Another of the problems here is that the legitimate sales of recorded music have not yet (as of 2001) turned down. The free exchange of that music is claimed to promote higher sales, though that belief will be tested if the recession continues.

3. What groups have been able to exercise their rights through the "free exchange" policy

Users of Napster say that they have a right to loan what they have purchased. They can loan cars, books and even clothes to other people; why cannot they loan music?

4. What groups have been denied their rights under the "free exchange" policy?

Producers of music, both artists and executives, say their work is intellectual property, and that they should own what they have created, or have paid others to create.

5. Express the moral problem so that every one will agree that their interests and rights have been recognized and included:

Is it right that students permit music they have purchased to be borrowed and then copied by others over the Internet, given that this generates much wider enjoyment of the music at much lower cost, and that the students clearly have a right to loan all other property they have purchased, but also given that the artists and the owners/ managers of recording companies receive reduced payments, and that this practice abridges the right of those artists and owner/managers to determine the use of their intellectual property?

6. What are the economic outcomes?

There is clearly a demand among students and other young people for borrowing and recording modern music, and there clearly is a supply of this modern music for borrowing and recording, but it is hard to think of these voluntary transactions as legitimate markets in that there are no cash payments and therefore no utility preferences. However, the legitimate markets for modern music that do exist, in which there are payments and preferences, do not seem to be fully competitive due to exclusive contracts between recording companies and the composing and performing artists. The buyers and the sellers in the voluntary exchanges seem fully informed, but there are also external costs imposed upon the owners and managers of the recording companies and the composting and performing artists of the music.

7. What are the legal requirements?

    The right of the buyers to use the music they have purchased as they wish, which is certainly a right they hold in regards to all other goods they may have purchased such as books, clothes and cars, conflicts with the right of the seller to limit that use in the case of intellectual, rather than physical, property. How to decide? My suggest is once again to come back to the "social contract" or "veil of ignorance" concepts. What would people who did not know whether they would be buyers or sellers decide?

8. What are the ethical duties?

    Personal virtues. Both the "buyers" of the music, who copy it from others, and the producers of the music, both artists and executives, appear to be open, honest and truthful about their acts. The copiers, however, may not be proud of their methods.

    Religious injunctions. Kindness and compassion do not seem to be issues here, but there certainly is no sense of community, nor any goal of common purpose, between the copiers and the producers.

    Utilitarian benefits. It is, for me, difficult to determine the net balance or "greatest good" between thecopiers' gain of benefits and the producers' loss of revenues generated by the free exchange of recorded music.

    Universal duties. It is necessary to distinguish between physical property and intellectual property; the same universal rules probably do not apply to both. Most people seem willing to loan physical property, if no damage is anticipated. Would most people be willing to loan intellectual property, if their income would be decreased?

    Distributive justice. The "least among us" in this situations probably are students, but it is hard to claim that they harmed by being denied the right to record borrowed music. That same music is freely available, though with less convenience, over the radio

    Contributive liberty. The same right to develop their skills to the fullest has to apply both to artists under contract with the recording studios, and those who would like to get better recognition in order to gain such a contract.

    What is my conclusion? I continually tell students in my classes that I am willing to express my opinion but that it remains just that: my opinion. It is not necessarily "right", and they are certainly at liberty to disagree as long as they can provide a supporting rationale for their opinion and their conclusion from economics, law and ethics. My thought here is 1) that these are non-market transactions, so they don't really "fit" under economic theory; 2) that these non-market transactions concern intellectual property where the law is not nearly as fully developed or widely accepted as with physical property so that the law doesn't really "fit' either; and 3) that the primary harms are financial in nature for musical artists and recording executives who appear to arouse little sympathy and seem to have plenty of money so that finally the ethical principles don't seem to "fit". The ethical principles here are ambiguous, as there are in the timeless question whether it is "right" for the parents of a starving baby to steal food from a rich family who will not miss it in the least.

There are not many moral issues that I consider to be a toss-up, but this is one of them. That sentiment seems to extend to my students. We generally take a vote at the end of the discussion of each case; this one usually divides 50/50.

Whirlpool Corporation and the Sale of Dish Antennas

This case works very well in my classes, but of course I am now teaching at the University of Alabama and the sale of the dish antennas occurred in rural Georgia, Alabama and Mississippi, and the trial that is described in the case took place in Greensboro, Alabama, 30 miles south of Tuscaloosa. Invariably one of the students in the class will say that his/her parents, grandparents or other relatives had purchased a dish antenna under the conditions described in the case, and he/she will explain how dissatisfied they eventually became with those conditions. Or, one of the students from the Greensboro area will add some further information about the trial. Fortunately, these revelations usually come about mid-way through the discussion, after sides have essentially been chosen, not right at the start when it could distort the discussion.

I do not divide up the class into groups for this case. Instead I conduct the class as a normal "what do you think about this action by this company?" discussion, but with a difference. I explain that you can be for Whirlpool or against Whirlpool, but that if you are for Whirlpool you must assume that you have been sent by that company to argue their position in front of the Board of Directors of the Southern Poverty Law Center, a very active non-governmental agency in Montgomery, Alabama that tends to support the residents of rural Alabama who believe that they have been economically exploited or legally deprived. If, on the other hand, you are against Whirlpool you must assume that you have been sent by the Southern Poverty Law Center to argue their position in front of the Board of Directors of Whirlpool Corporation in Benton Harbor, Michigan. In short, your task, as a member of the class, is to convince people who disagree with you, not just to express your thoughts.

I start by calling upon members of the class at random to make certain that everyone understands who is being benefited, who is being harmed, whose rights are being exercised and whose rights are being denied. I list those on the board, and – after that listing is complete – I go on to ask other students, "What do you think; which side are you on?" and list their arguments on the board under "for Whirlpool" and "against Whirlpool". For this note, however, I will use the same structure that I have used for the other case explanations:

1. What groups have benefited from the marketing and financing policies in the case?

Owners and managers of Whirlpool, from higher interest payments

Owners and managers of Gulf Coast Electronics, from higher sales levels
Customers of Whirlpool and Gulf Coast from better television reception

2. What groups have been harmed from the marking and financing policies in the case

Customers of Gulf Coast Electronics, from high sales prices ($1,124 vs $400)
Customers of Whirlpool, from high interest rates (22% rather than 10 to 12%
Residents of the rural South who have been targeted for aggressive sales

3. What groups were able to exercise their rights through these sales & financing policies?

Managers of Gulf Coast Electronics have a right to set prices on dish antennas
Managers of Whirlpool have a right to set interest rates on credit cards
Managers of both companies had a right to design aggressive sales campaign

4. What groups were unable to exercise their rights through these sales & financing policies?

Customers of Gulf Coast and Whirlpool had a right to truthful explanation of interest
Customers of Gulf Coast and Whirlpool had a right to be treated with dignity/respect

5. Express the moral problem so that everyone will believe that their moral concerns have been recognized and included:

Is it right that Gulf Coast and Whirlpool together aggressively market and finance television antennas in rural sections of the South given that this practice 1) financially benefits owners and managers of the two companies and markedly improves television reception for the customers, but also charges very high sales prices and interest rates for that improvement; and 2) recognizes the rights of company executives to set sales prices and interest rates, but denies the rights of customers to be told the truth about the interest rates and to receive prompt attention to their complaints?

6. What are the economic benefits?

There are competitive markets for both television dish antennas and consumer purchase financing, but the customers in this case appear to have been uninformed about those markets. It is certainly possible to argue that the customers should have visited a consumer electronics store to get better information about the antennas prices, but there seems to be no question but that they were misled about the financing rates. The concept that economic efficiency improves the full society requires informed customers, and when those customers are poorly educated perhaps extra care in providing that information is required.

7. What are the legal requirements?

The use of the "credit card for a single sale" form of consumer purchase financing fits within a niche – or, some would say loophole – of the financing laws. It makes possible a combination of the low down payments and the high interest rates that go with credit cards and the large amounts that go with installment loans. The only way to look at these "on the edge of legality" loans is to attempt to envisage what the law would be if the people developing that law did not know whether they would be executives in the loan company earning substantial interest rates and late payment fees, or the people who were able to purchase major products or home improvements through those loans.

8. What are the ethical duties

Personal virtues. Can the executives at Whirlpool be open, honest, truthful and proud of these loans. They apparently were not truthful about the interest rates.

Religious injunctions. Are these loans kind and compassionate, and do they create a sense of community, of the finance company and the rural consumers joining together in pursuit of a common goal?

Utilitarian benefits. It is hard, for me, to envisage the "greater good" here. The rural poor do have improved TV reception, but at a cost of high interest rates and late fees.

Universal duties. Would the executives at Whirlpool want to be misled about the terms of their home mortgages or investment accounts?

Distributive justice. The "least among us" in this instance are the rural poor; the question is whether they are harmed by paying large amounts for better TV reception.

Contributive liberty. It is possible to make the argument that the interest rates and late fees detract from the rural customer's ability to develop their skills to the fullest, but it is necessary to recognize that they did make this choice themselves

What happened? The jury returned a verdict in favor of the three plaintiffs for $580 million. The defendant, Whirlpool Corporation, appealed that award to the judge in the trial court, who reduced it to $300 million but said that he had seldom seen actions by a large corporation so exploitive of poor and uneducated customers. Whirlpool then appealed this new amount to the state Supreme Court, but reached a settlement with the plaintiff's attorneys before that court rendered a verdict. The amount of the settlement remains confidential. Whirlpool, however, apparently was embarrassed by the publicity associated with the trial and by the actions of its customer finance division. They sold the Whirlpool Financial National Bank, the portion of that division that had negotiated the "single purchase credit card" loans to purchase satellite dish antennas, to a West Coast financial institution.

One of the conditions of the sale of Whirlpool Financial National Bank was that the West Coast financial institution did not have to transfer any of the employees. They did not do so, and everyone associated with those single purchase credit card loans, which generated such high profits, was essentially fired. I use this to explain to the students, at the conclusion of the class, that you are not necessarily protected if you remain silent at work when you encounter what you consider to be a moral problem. Whistle-blowers traditionally are disliked by their employers, but nonwhistle-blowers can encounter problems also. It's all a matter of where you "draw the line".

I usually conclude this class with a mini-lecture (10 to 15 minutes) showing how this case fits within the analytical framework of the course, and how that framework helps to decide where to draw the line. I end by asking them to apply this framework to the next case or cases, with particular attention to the "economic outcome" argument (expressed in Chapter II) that adherence to market forces improves the wellbeing of overall society. I mention those cases by name, and describe their moral problems briefly, and then quit.

Teaching Notes for Chapter II –Moral Analysis and Economic Outcomes

The basic theme of this chapter is that it is not possible to rely totally on the economic concept of Pareto Optimality in making decisions which result in an increase in the well being of some, and a decrease in the well being of others. The economic argument is that these increases and decreases are the result of individual buy and sell decisions in impersonal product and factor markets, and that as long as business firms attempt to produce the most needed products with the least valued resources, then the full society will be as well off as possible. Any lasting harms, the economic argument continues, can be remedied by political, not financial, procedures.

People select what they most want, the economic argument continues, from impersonal product markets to obtain the goods and service they need to live. People also give up what they least want in impersonal factor markets (labor, material and capital) to gain the income they need to purchase those goods and services. If everyone is purchasing what they most want with the income gained from selling the resources (including their own time) that they least want, then as long as business firms are operating as efficiently as possible (maximizing revenues and mini-mizing costs) no one can be made better off unless there are non-market transactions through personal gifts or governmental programs. Transactions in these impersonal markets will result in a situation where the overall well being of the full society is at the highest point possible for no one person can be made better off without harming some other person, as long as members of the producing and distributing sectors of the economy (the business firms) act to maximize revenues, minimize costs and consequently optimize profits within the constraints of those markets.

The economic argument, then, is that there are two responsibilities of the managers of business firms: 1) to optimize profits within the constraints of the product and factor markets' and 2) ensure that those markets are competitive, that their customers (product markets) and their suppliers (factor markets), are informed, and that their external costs (costs imposed by the com-pany, not negotiated through the markets) are included in the sales prices of their goods and ser-vices. There has always been confusion about this economic argument among non-economists because the first "optimize profits" requirement has been loudly emphasized while the second "but of course at the same time maintain competitive markets, inform market participants, and include external costs" has been quietly assumed. A copy of the conceptual structure of this full economic argument that impersonal product and factor markets for customers and suppliers lead towards Pareto Optimal conditions for the full society (Figure #2-2 from Chapter II) is given on the following page, in type large enough to be reproduced for a vue-graph slide to be used in classroom lectures/discussions.

The counter argument is that microeconomic theory makes assumptions about the nature of human beings, and the worth of human beings, that need correction by meeting legal require-ments (decisions by the full society) and observing ethical duties (principles for a good society). In short, the argument of this book is that it is necessary to use all three analytical methods (mar-ket forces, legal requirement and ethical duties) for the analysis of moral problems in which there are mixtures of benefits and harms, and conflicts between rights recognized and rights ignored, for different groups of people at different periods of time. That is the content, in very summary

Conceptual Structure of Microeconomic Theory

Consumers, whose marginal utilities for a mix of goods and services can be expressed as individual demand curves Product markets for goods and services, with aggregate demand and supply curves that determine prices to be charged

Overall well being of society dependent upon market forces, but modified by a political process for a partial redistribution of income to consumers and public agencies within society

Producing firms, whose marginal costs determine a company's supply curve for goods and services and whose marginal productivity rates determine company demand curves for the various input factors

Owners of land and capital, whose supplies are fixed over the short term, and workers whose marginal utility for income limits the labor supply, also over the short term

Factor markets for material, labor and capital, with aggregate demand and supply curves that determine the factors to be used and the prices to be charged.

form, of Chapter II. The question is how to get that content across to students, and here I have three suggestions:

1. Assignment questions. Here is a set of assignment questions. As explained previously (in the note to Chapter I) I don't use them because I think that students should be able to get the essential meaning from a reading without hints or suggestion as to where they should focus. And, I think that if the students anticipate that the class the next day will just constitute a discussion followed by a lecture about those assignment questions they will not read the text with adequate care and attention the previous night. You may disagree, so here are some questions that do – in my view – get to the heart of microeconomic theory as a moral "best for society" precept:

    > How would you explain the economic rationale of the famous quotation by Milton Friedman that is given in Chapter II, on page 34? Prof. Friedman writes that, "Few trends could so thoroughly undermine the very foundations of our free society as the acceptance by corporate officials of a social responsibility other than to make as much money for their stockholders as possible"

    > How would you apply microeconomic theory and the concept of Pareto Optimality to the three issues that were used to introduce the nature of ethics in management on the first page of Chapter I?

    > > The executives who happened to hold duplicate positions following a merger, and consequently were to be victims of "downsizing".

    > > The wholesalers who helped to successfully establish a new product, but now represent a much more costly means of reaching the market.

    > > The dam, which is to be built on private land, but which will block a river used by local residents and summer vacationers for years.

    > Milton Friedman has the reputation of being both brusque and bright. Suppose, as part of a national program for college students on the topic of the social responsibility of business firms, he agreed to listen to you for 5 minutes. What would you say?

2. Start-up suggestions. I would recommend strongly that you start the class that will take up the economic arguments of Chapter II with the short "greed is good" speech from *Wall Street*. The setting is the annual meeting of the stockholders of a large paper manufacturer that Gordon Ghecko wishes to acquire in an unfriendly take-over. He defends his actions with, essentially, the economic efficiency rationale of Milton Friedman. The speech is short. The setting is realistic. And, the conclusion – greater economic efficiency will help this tired old giant (remember, this film dates from the 1980s), the United States of America – is dramatic.

    My students like films and videos in the classroom, and they particularly like this one, even though many have not seen it before. Their conclusion usually is that greed is good within limits. They always have a difficult time defining those limits, but they usually don't disagree when I suggest that the only limits that are possible are external (our obedience to the laws of our society) and internal (our recognition of the duties we owe to our society). I then move on to the case or cases for the day, often having small 4-person in-class discussion groups prepare vue-graph reports, as described earlier, for presentation to the rest of the class

Susan Shapiro and Workplace Safety

The woman given the disguised name of Susan Shapiro was a member of one of my corporate strategy classes at the University of Michigan. The background given in the case is accurate. She had served in the Israeli army. She did have a degree in chemistry from Smith, and a masters in chemical engineering from M.I.T, and she did go to work for a large chemical company very soon after graduation. During the first month of her employment she was taken on a trip, with other recent management hires, to visit a chemical plant in Louisiana. She immediately recognized what she felt was a very dangerous situation: benzene, a known carcinogen, was being used to "wash" (remove surface impurities) a chemical product. This was being done in the open air, in a shed with a metal roof, so that it was technically legal, but the fume concentrations under that roof were far above federal standards. She complained to the plant manager, who said that he recognized the problem but had been unable to get the investment funds needed to change the process. When Susan said that she would go back to corporate headquarters and try to get those funds, the plant manager asked Susan not to get him involved

I look upon this as a "where do you draw the line" case. Susan, within the first month of her employment, has encountered a situation that, the plant manager warned, could threaten her employment with the firm. I generally start the discussion by asking why the plant manager is so pusillanimous, so hesitant for push for a process improvement that he knows would improve plant safety and assist worker health. I would hope that members of your class would recognize that it is very much easier to suggest forceful actions to solve moral problems when you are a young student at college rather than a middle-aged manager at work. Middle-aged managers at work have multiple obligations – mortgages on their family's home and savings for their children's education – that we all know middle-aged persons in all occupations tend to accumulate over time.

I would also hope that members of your class would recognize that this hesitancy to get involved is one of the problems of large diverse companies in globally competitive industries. People at corporate headquarters in New York City who approve/disapprove requests for funding from chemical plants in Louisiana do not see the conditions or smell the fumes at those plants, and they do not know and like the workers affected by those conditions and those fumes. One of the basic truisms of managerial ethics is that it is hard for corporate level managers to be sympathetic for people they don't really know. After you get these "why people don't want to get involved" thoughts across I would suggest that you go on to your normal discussion method, helped – I hope – by the following outline:

1. What groups will be benefited if the present "open air" benzene process is continued?

    Owners of the company will have reduced investments and higher profits

Managers of the company will have lower costs and higher bonuses
Workers in the company will have a more competitive firm and more secure jobs

2. What groups will be harmed if the present "open air" benzene process is continued?

Entry level employees may become ill from the carcinogenic chemical
Children of those employees may suffer birth defects from the chemical.

3. What groups will be able to fully exercise their rights if the present process is continued?

Owners have the right to maximize profits within the law
Managers have the right to select the best chemical process within the law

4. What groups will be denied some of their rights if the present process is continued?

Entry level employees have the right to a safe workplace
Future children of those employees have the right to a healthy life

5. Express the moral problems so that everyone involved will believe that their particular interests have been recognized and included.

Is it "right" that the chemical company continue the existing "open air" benzene process, given that it generates lower costs and higher profits and is a legally permissible design, but also given that the definite exposure to high concentrations of benzene may result in health care problems for exposed workers and their unborn children?

6. What are the economic benefits?

There is no question but that the "open air" benzene process is low investment and consequently low costs, but the entry level workers (participants in the input factor market for labor) are not fully informed, and essentially future he health care problems are being forced onto those workers as an external cost

7. What are the legal requirements?

There is no question but that the "open air" benzene process is currently legal, but there also is no question but that one of the goals of workplace safety law is to protect workers from exposure to harmful concentrations of carcinogenic chemicals. What would people who did not know if they were wealthy owners or entry level workers decide?

8. What are the ethical duties?

Personal virtues. The owners and managers have not been open and truthful about the possible consequences of this problem, and would not want to see that problem and/or those consequences widely reported in national newspapers

Religious injunctions. This action is not kind and compassionate, and does not create a sense of community between owners, managers, workers and customers, in pursuit of a common goal.

Utilitarian benefits. The "greatest good for the greatest number" is unclear. The increased profits can easily be computed; the health damages to workers and children hard to rd to estimate.

Universal duties. Would the owners of the company want this level of exposure to benzene in their homes, or would the executives permit this level of exposure to potentially harmful chemicals in their offices?

Distributive justice. The entry level workers, and/or their unborn children, are clearly the least among us in this situation, and they are being harmed.

Contributive liberty. The entry level workers, and/or their children, will be prevented from developing their skills to the fullest if they become ill

9. What happened? Members of my class always say that Susan should return to New York City, the headquarters of the chemical company, write a report, pass it through channels, and assume that the process improvements would then be funded. Susan did go back to New York, did write the report, did pass it through channels, and nothing happened. Susan then went to see the president of the company. He listened patiently, said that the situation could not be as bad as she had described but promised that he would "look into the matter" anyway. Six months passed, and again nothing happened. She tried to see the president a second time, but he refused. Susan sent her report, together with a covering letter, to the Occupational Safety and Health Administration in Washington, with copies to the New York Times, Washington Post and New Orleans Times/Picayune. She was fired the next day.

    OSHA investigated, and found that more than a hundred of the employees who at one time had worked at the benzene washing process had latter become ill with various forms of cancer, and that many of their children had been affected. The company was fined millions of dollars by OSHA, and the harmed employees and their children sued for millions more. The president, who had ignored Susan's warnings and then refused to meet with her, was fired. Susan, however, felt that she was blacklisted by other chemical companies, and even consulting firms and investment banks. She now lives and works in Israel.

World Bank and the Export of Pollution

This case presents the economic arguments for Pareto Optimality in exceedingly stark terms: the United States and other industrially developed nations should move pollution producing industries overseas, to 3rd world countries, because people in those countries have lower economic expectations for their lives and lower economic values for their environments. In short, it costs less to bring about the death of a person in a 3rd world country because the value of that life can be computed by discounting back to net present value the future stream of that person's annual wages. If those wages are lower, then the value of that life is lower. My students generally understand this very critical assumption, but they don't like to talk about it at the start of class so I don't force them to do so. Instead, I try to make it easier for them by going directly to the standard analysis methodology recommended in this text:

1. What groups will be benefited by exporting pollution causing industries to 3rd world countries?

    Residents of 1st world countries, who will not have pollution
    Workers in 3rd world countries who will have jobs
    Residents in 3rd world countries who will have economic development and –probably – tax payments by the pollution causing industries
    Owners and managers of pollution causing industries in 1st world countries who will not have government imposed expenses to reduce the pollution

2. What groups will be harmed by exporting pollution causing industries to 3rd world counties

    Residents of 3rd world countries, whose health and possibly life will definitely be affected
    Workers in 1st world countries who will lose their jobs
    Persons throughout the world, for the total air and water pollution will increase

3. What groups will be able to exercise their rights by exporting pollution causing industries?

    Owners and managers of pollution causing industries have a right to select the location if the amount and type of pollution is legal in the 3rd world country
    Employees in the 3rd world country have a right to work, again if the amount and type of pollution is legal in that country

4. What groups will be denied their rights by exporting pollution causing industries?

    Residents of the 3rd world country who have a right to health that will be denied
    Residents of the 3rd world country also have a right to vote that frequently is denied in these non-democratic nations; they will have no say in the acceptance of the pollution

5. Express the moral problem so that everyone involved will believe that their particular interests (their well being and their rights) have been recognized and included

    Is it "right" that pollution causing industries be exported from 1st world to 3rd world countries, given that residents in the 1st world nations will be benefited by the lack of pollution and workers in 3rd world nations by the presence of jobs, but also given that workers in 1st world nations will lose their jobs, workers and residents in 3rd world nations will have their health affected, and inhabitants of the world generally will have to endure greater pollution. The owners and managers of the pollution causing companies have a right to select a location for their plants as long as those plants meet local laws, but residents of the 3rd world nations also should have a right to determine the nature of those laws.

6. What are the economic outcomes?

Prof. Summers and his supporter, Prof. Landsburg, are absolutely correct in their economic reasoning. As long as the factor owners in the 3rd world nations, the workers and residents, prefer additional jobs and taxes to environmental deterioration and poor health, then it is economically permissible for companies to move the pollution causing processes to those locations. But, it is highly questionable if the factor markets in those countries are fully competitive, if the factor owners are fully informed about the health consequences, and if the external costs imposed upon the residents of those countries are fully included in the sale prices of the final products.

7. What are the legal requirements?

It is generally illegal in the United States to export pollution (toxic wastes in solid or liquid form), but it is legal in the United States to export, or move overseas, pollution causing processes. It is legal in most 3rd world countries to operate pollution causing processes without environmental controls, but those laws are seldom the result of democratic methods. The only way to resolve such a conflict is to attempt to imagine what people, who did not know whether they would be workers for the companies and/or members of the ruling class, both of whom would benefit, or residents, most of whom would be harmed, would decide.

8. What are the ethical duties?

Personal virtues. It is questionable how open, honest and truthful most of the 3rd world countries have been about the acceptance of pollution causing industries. It is also questionable how proud the owners and managers of those pollution causing companies have been about their movements abroad

Religious injunctions. Is the movement of pollution causing processes to 3rd world countries kind and compassionate? Does it create a sense of community, of 1st world and 3rd world members working jointly for a common goal? My answer to both is "no" at the present, but it could be "yes" if there were greater control of the pollution

Utilitarian benefits. It is easy to measure the financial benefits of increased jobs and greater taxes in the 3rd world countries. It is hard to measure the environmental harms to the health of workers and residents in those countries.

Universal duties. Would the owners and managers of pollution causing industries in the United States want 3rd world companies to bring their harmful methods, such as the employment of child labor, to the United States if the owners and managers had no say in the laws controlling those practices?

Distributive justice. Here is it not clear exactly what groups constitutes the "least among us" If they are the unemployed persons in the 3rd world who would now have jobs, then they are benefited. If they are the residents of those countries who might suffer damage to their health, then they would be harmed.

Contributive liberty. This principle is also ambiguous. The unemployed in the 3rd world are able to develop their skills, and maximize their opportunities for a full life. The residents of those countries, if they become ill, would be unable to develop their skills and fulfill their lives.

Lawrence Summers went on to become Secretary of the Treasury in the Clinton administration, and recently (2001) was appointed president of Harvard University. He has apologized for his famous memo, which he said did not and does not reflect his full thinking. But that memo does reflect economic theory in its most stark form. My thought is that a good way to wind up this class is not with the memo, but with the anecdote about converting wildness into parking lots provided by Prof. Landsburg, at the end of the case:

.....The conflict arises because each side wants to allocate the same resource in a different way. Jack wants his woodland at the expense of Jill's parking [lot] and Jill wants her parking [lot] at the expense of Jacks' woodland.

I explain to the students that Jill can obviously make a profit by paving over the forest, providing there is a demand for parking in the area (perhaps the woodland in question is within easy viewing distance of an attractive waterfall). The question I then ask the students is whether this decision, which will affect all of us, should be made by Jill and Jack just by optimizing their economic interests, or whether there should be some consideration by both to the legal requirements of the society and to their ethical duties to the society.

Green Giant and the Move to Mexico

There is a 20 minute videotape available on the decision of the Green Giant company to move their frozen food production from Salinas, California to Irapuato, Mexico. The company moved, as was explained in the case, from a wage rate of $7.50 per hour to a wage rate of $0.65 per hour, though at a social cost to the people in Salinas (joblessness) and an environmental cost to the people in Irapuato (water depletion). The videotape was produced at the University of Michigan. I have since moved to the University of Alabama, and there are no procedures in place in Ann Arbor to distribute that tape. If you would like a copy, contact me here in Tuscaloosa, at (205) 348-8931 or LHosmer@cba.uia.edu; there will be no charge.

Green Giant is a food products company that specializes in canned and frozen vegetables. Started in Minnesota in 1903, it was one of the first to adopt a memorable advertising character, the Jolly Green Giant who, together with his friend Little Sprout, appeared at first in magazines, then on radio, and eventually on television. The company was also among the first to begin producing frozen vegetables.

In the 1960s the company was moved to Salinas, California, 30 miles inland from Monterey. This was an area of fertile farmland with an agricultural workforce composed largely of recent emigrants from Mexico. By 1990, the date of the case, the company employed about 2,000 people within the area, many of whom had been with the company for 20 to even 30 years. Most had not learned English, or been trained for higher level jobs.

In 1990 Green Giant was acquired by the Grand Metropolitan Company of Great Britain in an unfriendly takeover. Executives at Green Giant were told that, to help pay off the debt arising from the acquisition, profits had to be increased quickly. It was inferred that Green Giant managers had gotten old and stodgy, and they needed to get lean and mean. Grand Metropolitan was explicit in saying that their management style was a "light but firm hand upon the throat".

The problem for the managers of Green Giant was that it would be difficult to increase profits quickly. The frozen vegetables industry is mature, with limited growth and lots of competition. Green Giant had the best known trademark and the biggest market share, but they still controlled only 14% of total industry sales. 86% was held by other large companies that would not give up their market shares easily.

There was one way to increase profits quickly. It would be possible to move all operations from Salinas, California where the wage rate was $7.50/hour to Irapuato, Mexico where the wage rate was $0.65 hour. Irapuato is in central Mexico, far south of the border; it is an area with a hot, sunny climate and dry fertile soil that produces excellent vegetable crops. It is also an area with a surplus labor supply.

Green Giant operated a small processing plant in the Irapuato, and so was familiar with the advantages, and with the problems, of the proposed move. The main problem was a shortage of water. Green Giant would have to drill a well 450' deep to get adequate clean water to wash the vegetables prior to freezing. It was expected that a well this deep would dry up the 20' and 30" wells of the local population, who would then be forced to get water for cooking and washing from the river which was polluted with sewage discharged directly into the river by other towns and villages upstream. It is said that the Mexican people have developed resistance to the organisms in sewage polluted river water, but there would still be serious illnesses, especially among very young children and very old adults. The town of Irapuato had a small municipal water system that purified river water, but it served only the commercial center of town and there was no money for an expensive expansion project.

Another problem in Irapuato was the shortage of farm land. It would be necessary to convert about 6,000 acres of farm land from growing corn and beans, the local subsistence crops, to growing broccoli and cauliflower for Green Giant to freeze, package and export. The area land owners wold be pleased to have this new market for their produce, but the local people would be forced to pay higher prices for their food. The transportation and distribution systems in rural Mexico are not very developed; it would be difficult to bring in food from other regions.

The loss of 2,000 jobs, and the resulting unemployment, would be devastating to the workers and the economy of Salinas, California. The workers there were neither well educated nor well trained; it would be hard to them to find other work. Green Giant was also the largest tax payer in Salinas; it would be hard for that city to find other sources of revenue.

1. What groups will be benefited, and how much, by the move to Irapuato?

Stockholders in Grand Metropolitan, who will save $13,200/worker, or $26.4 million/yr.

Managers in Green Giant, who will deliver a profit increase and keep their jobs/bonuses
Workers in Irapuato, who will have jobs at $0.65/hr, above the minimum wage of $0.55
Customers in the United States, if prices for frozen foods are lowered

2. What groups will be harmed, and how badly, by the move to Irapuato?

Workers in Salinas, who will lose jobs after 20 to – in a few instances – 30 years
Residents in Salinas, who will have to make up lost tax revenues
Residents in Irapuato, who will have to get and use river water, after their well dry up
Consumers in Irapuato, who will have to pay higher prices for corn and beans

3. Whose rights will be exercised, and made more certain, by the move to Irapuato?

Stockholders in Grand Metropolitan have a right to make managers strive for legal profits
Managers in Green Giant have a right to position the company's production legally

4. Whose rights will be infringed, or made less certain, by the mover to Irapuato?

Workers in Salinas; they <u>may</u> have a right to their jobs after 20 to 30 years
Residents in Irapuato; they <u>may</u> have a right to the water in their wells
Consumers in Irapuato; they <u>may</u> have a right to the food grown on local lands

5. State the moral problem:

Is it right that Green Giant move from Salinas, California to Irapuato, Mexico, which will result in substantially higher profits for the stockholders in Great Britain and far more jobs for the workers in Irapuato, but will also result in a loss of jobs and increase in taxes for the people in Salinas and a loss of well water and higher food prices for people in Irapuato.

6. What are the economic outcomes?

There clearly is a factor market for labor in Irapuato, and the company plans to pay market wages. Those wages may seem low to some of us, but they have been set by the market, not by the company. There is also a market for farm produce in Irapuato, and again Green Giant plans to pay market prices . This may drive up the prices for corn and beans, but again an economist would say that is the result of market actions, not company actions. Lastly, there is a market for frozen broccoli and cauliflower in the United State, and the company plans to charge market prices. In brief, this situation is economically efficient, except for the external costs imposed upon the residents of Irapuato by the taking of their well water.

7. What are the legal requirements?

In the United States there clearly is no law against closing a plant. There are some laws about notification of the closing and continuation of benefits, but it can be assumed that

Green Giant plans to fully follow those laws. In Mexico there are some laws about minimum wages, but apparently none about overtime hours, and again it can be assumed that the company plans to follow those laws. There apparently is not law against drilling a deeper well, and taking the well water of others with shallower wells, But the democratic process in Mexico is notoriously manipulated; it is not altogether clear that the lack of such a law reflects a lack of popular desire for such a law. My suggestion is once again to come back to the "social contract" and/or "veil of ignorance" concepts; what would people who did not know whether they would be Grand Metropolitan stockholders or Irapuato residents decide?

8. What are the ethical duties?

Personal virtues. Green Giant has not been open about and cannot be proud of many of the consequences of this move: the low wages, long hours and dried –up wells in Irapuato and the discharge of long-service employees in Salinas.

Religious injunctions. There seems to be little kindness and compassion, and there also appears to be no sense of community, of everyone in both the United States and Mexico working for a common goal.

Utilitarian benefits. The loss of jobs and tax payments in Salinas and the gain of jobs and tax payment in Irapuato would seem to cancel each other out. The net balance of good over harm would seem to depend upon the cost assigned to the lost well water.

Universal dues. It can be assumed that the executives at Green Giant and at Grand Metropolitan would grudgingly agree that their jobs could be ended by a major cost cutting effort. It is less certain that they would agree that their water supply could be taken.

Distributive justice. It would seem that there are two groups of the "least among us" in this case: the discharged workers in Salinas and the local residents in Irapuato. Both are being harmed.

Contributive liberty. It is hard for me to say that anyone's ability to develop their skills to the fullest has been diminished. It will be hard for the ex-workers in Salinas to train themselves for other work, but that is not the direct result of Green Giant's action.

What happened? Green Giant did move. There were popular protests in Salinas, and adverse publicity was generated on the national level, but there were no customer boycotts of the company's products in the United States nor worker slowdowns at the company's plants in Mexico. My suggestion is that at the end of the class you discuss some of the actions Green Giant might have taken to mitigate the most direct of the harms caused by their move to Irapuato. Those might include a substantial contribution to the expansion and modernization of the water treatment plant in Irapuato, and/or a substantial contribution towards the retraining and new placement of the workers in Salinas

Teaching Notes for Chapter III – Moral Analysis and Legal Requirements

The basic argument of this chapter is that it is not possible to rely totally upon the law in making decisions that result in positive outcomes for some against negative outcomes for others, or that recognize the rights of some and ignore the rights of others. The law is a set of rules, established by society, to govern behavior within that society, and that behavior certainly includes outcomes and rights. Why not, then, let the law decide, particularly in a democratic society where the argument can easily be made that the law represents a set of the collective moral judgments held by members of society. The problem is that this "democratically enacted law equals collectively held standards" argument does not hold up. The social and political process by which individual moral standards that guide personal conduct are coalesced into the legal rules that govern societal behavior are flawed. There is some overlap between the moral standards of the members of society and the legal requirements of the full society, but that overlap is far from complete. A graphic of that process (Figure #3-3 from Chapter III) is given on the following page, in type large enough to be reproduced for a vue-graph slide to be used in classroom lectures/discussion.

1. Assignment questions. Once again, I do not often use assignment questions in my classes because I find that they don't "work" for me and are generally ignored in the preparation of my students. I have an assignment project, however, for Chapter III that does seem to work and is not ignored, probably because the students seem interested in the outcome of the assignment, which shows the average or typical values of the other members of the class. The questionnaire for that project is given on page #3 of this note in a form that can easily be reproduced and distributed. I stress in making this assignment that the questionnaire is to be anonymous; students are not to put their names on their papers. I also ask that the papers be handed in, or that the values be recorded on a home page, the day before we are to discuss Chapter III in class so that averages can be computed.

I add up the responses, in a reverse order of significance (similar to a golf game, the low score "wins") with a "1" for the most important value for each student and a "12" for the least important. In the discussion I ask what most people would think would be the order of importance among students at a business school; that is, what is the stereotype of business students. The response generally is that it would essentially be the order in which the values are listed, with #1, "increases in wealth, and the power, possessions & life style that go with money": would lead, with #12 "peace between nations, and a lack of oppression of the people living on the earth" would be at the end. There is, of course, considerable variation, but in my classes #5, "attention to my family", usually leads, with #2, "advancement in my company" second and #11 "preservation of the environment" third.

2. Start-up suggestions. If you wish to focus on the reading, and not use the assignment project explained above, then I would recommend that you start the class discussion by putting on a vue graph the following quotation from page 61 of the text:

The analytical method of legal requirements can be summarized very simply in the statement that everyone should always obey the law. The law in a democratic society can

42

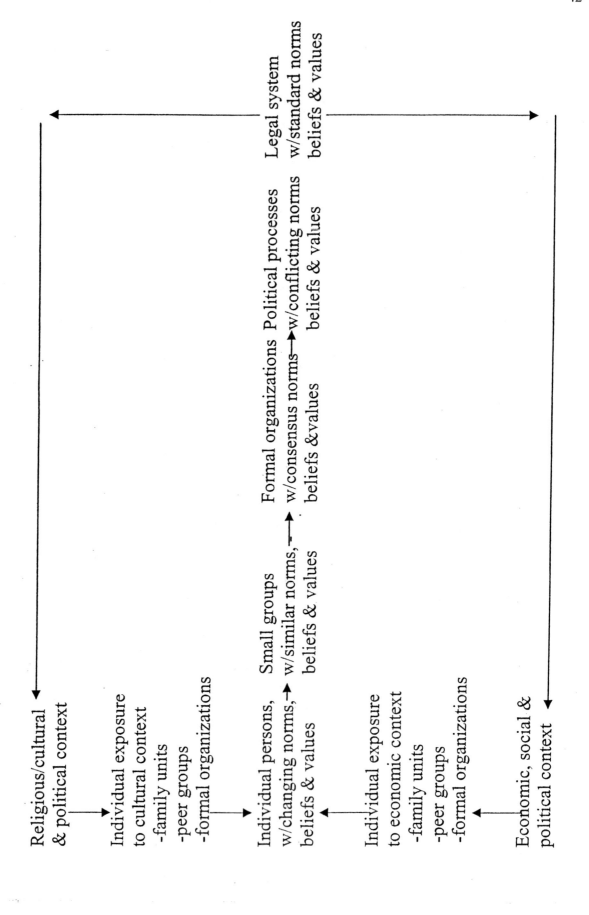

Class Assignment on Personal Goals, Norms, Beliefs and Values

Start to think about your own goals, norms, beliefs and values. You will not be forced to discuss these in class; it would obviously be inappropriate to call upon a person and ask, "What are your basic values, what do you feel is most important in your life?" But, think about your goals, your norms, you beliefs and your values, all as defined in Chapter III in the text.

Values, of course, are priorities among those goals, norms and beliefs. Below you will find a list of 12 statements, each of which implies a given goal. Rank these statements in your order of importance; that is, from 1 for the highest in your preference to 12 for the lowest. Hand in those rankings with no name attached so that anonymous totals for the class can be computed.

1. Increased in my wealth, and the power, possessions & life style that go with money, are important to me.

2. Advancement in my company, and the authority & prestige that go with promotion, are important to me.

3. Performance in may job, and the security & respect that go with achievement, are important to me.

4. Reputation within my community, and the political influences & social activities and go with reputation, are important to me.

5. Attention to my family, and the affecti0n & companionship that go with family life, are important to me.

6. Devotion to my church, and the sense of community & sharing that are part of most religions, are important to me

7. Independence in my life, and the ability to achieve may own goals and follow my own rules (as long as I do not directly harm others, or interfere with their rights) are important to me.

8. Interdependence with my fellow citizens, and the opportunity to set social goals and adopt mutual rules (though democratic processes) are important to me

9. Protection of the poor, and the chance to help others within our society who have been less fortunate than I, are important to me.

10. Equality among genders, races and ethnic groups, and the need to achieve courtesy and/or respect between peoples, are important to me

11. Preservation of the environment, and a lack of exploitation of the earth's resources, are important to me.

12. Peace between nations, and a lack of oppression of the people living upon this earth, are both important to me.

be said to represent the minimal moral standards of that society, and those minimal moral standards should recognize the nature and understand the worth of individual human beings. You may or may not agree with the extent of those standards, or the degree of that recognition and understanding, but – the legal argument continues -- you cannot really fault a person who obeys the law. You may feel that a person within an organization who faces a complex moral problem in which some people are going to be harmed and harmed badly, or have their rights eroded and eroded harshly, should go beyond the law. That person, however, may disagree with you. He or she may say, "We plan to optimize returns for our firm and benefits for our society. If you don't like that outcome, get together with a majority of your fellow citizens and pass a new law, which more fully recognizes the nature and understands the worth of other people, and we will obey the provisions of that new law. But, until that happens please do not lecture us on the superiority of your moral standards. We see nothing wrong with what we are doing, and evidently other people don't either for what we are doing is currently legal and approved by a majority of the population."

Then, I would suggest that you ask the following questions to ensure that members of the class understand the basic implausibility of the beliefs stated in that paragraph. If you don't follow through now, and ensure understanding of the lack of a direct relationship between moral standards and legal requirements, you will find when you get to more complex matters in the next few chapter that some members of the class will be sure to say, "It's not against the law", as if that totally settled the matter.

Why is this view that laws represent the combined moral judgments of members of our society) popular among many people? My answer is that it is so popular because it is so simple and direct, and offers a basis for choice that can be ascribed to others without accepting responsibility oneself. "I don't like it but it's the law" is an easy evasion of responsibility.

Can people in the class think of situations that are clearly not illegal and yet can easily be seen to be unethical. My response here would include water and air pollution before passage of the various pollution control laws as one example, and racial, gender or age discrimination before passage of civil rights legislation as another. My suggestion is that you spend some time here. You want to firmly get across the idea that just because a practice is legal, it is not necessarily "right", and may very well indeed be obviously "wrong".

3. Discussion issues. As described in the "Suggestions" part of this teaching guide, I often assign two cases for one class, with one case for the front of the room and one for the back, and I often break up those portions of the room into small groups of four students, and given them 20 minutes to meet and prepare a report to the balance of the class on what should be done regarding the moral problem in "their" case. That truly does seem to work well. I recommend it highly. Now, on to an outline of the three cases that followed Chapter III:

Sarah Goodwin and Consumer Protection

The woman given the disguised name of Sarah Goodwin was a member of one of my corporate strategy classes at Stanford; I held a visiting appointment there for one year a number of years ago. She must hold some sort of record for the shortest full time employment of any of their graduates. She graduated from the MBA program in May, took two months off to travel in Europe, started in a management training program at a large department store chain in August, and was fired in September.

All of the new employees in that training program were assigned to work with one of the buyers in the largest and most prestigious store in the chain. Sarah went to work for the buyer in charge of gourmet foods. After just a few weeks she was instructed by that buyer to arrange to ship some tainted food products to a convenience store chain that operated in one of the poorer sections of Los Angeles. "Ship it to the ghetto", she was told, and given the telephone number of the convenience store person to call to arrange for that shipment, "They can sell anything. We've got to get our money back"

Members of my class always say, if I don't break them up into groups, that Sarah should refuse to make the shipment and then, if the buyer continues to insist that she do so, that Sarah should report this incidence to the president of the chain or the vice president managing the store. The earlier example of Susan Shapiro (case following Chapter II), who reported a moral problem to the president of a chemical company, and was fired, evidently doesn't convince them that whistle-blowers are not appreciated. My students seem to start this case with the assumption that if you report moral wrong-doing anywhere (except maybe a chemical company) the situation will be corrected with no harm to the individual.

That may not be true in this instance. Maria, the supervisor and mentor, is described in the case as a person who is "witty, competent and sarcastic", and who serves as "sounding board, consultant and friend" to all of the other buyers. Sarah has to find a position with one of those buyers at the end of a four week stint with Maria to continue in the training program. The possibility of ostracism always seems to be clear to at least one person in every "break out" or "case discussion" group. That is one of the reasons I use those groups. If you fear that this will not happen, and that the possibility of ostracism is not clear, then during the early "set the stage" discussion of benefits and harms I suggest you ask specifically, "What will happen if Sarah blows the whistle and reports Maria to the store manager or the company president?" My argument is that Sarah must come out with a convincing moral solution, and the way to do that is to go through the full analytical procedure (Figure 1-1 in Chapter I) that forms the structure of this text:

Before breaking up into groups, if you plan to follow that recommendation, or before starting the discussion in the full class, I suggest that you read to the class the last paragraph of the case, which is the defense offered by Maria:

> I [Sarah] protested, but Maria told me, "Look, there is nothing wrong with this. The people down in the ghetto have never had luxury food items of this nature. These wafers will be sold very cheaply, and for most of the people who buy them it will be an opportunity

to try something really good. Only a few people will get an infested box. They won't be very happy, but down in the ghetto they expect that when they see a low price on an expensive product. They make the choice. We don't.

1. What groups will be benefited by shipping the defective wafers to the inner city?

   Owners and mangers of the department store chain will have increased returns
   Maria Castellani (the buyer) will have higher profits for her department. Buyers at this department store chain are measured on profits per square foot of selling space.

2. What groups will be harmed by shipping the defective wafers to the inner city?

   Customers of the convenience store chain who will be sold an infested food product
   Managers of the convenience store chain, I assume, know that there is something wrong with the discount goods provided, and consequently can't really be said to be harmed

3. What groups will be able to exercise their rights by shipping the defective wafers

   It is hard for me to think of any legitimate right exercised by those making this shipment

4. What groups will have their right ignored by this shipment

   Customers of the convenience store chain have a right to wholesome food products
   Residents of the inner city have a right to be treated with dignity and respect

5. Express the moral problem so that everyone involved will believe that their particular interests (their well being and their rights) have been recognized and included:

   Is it "right" that the department store chain ship a a partially infested food product for sale to customers in the ghetto, given that owners, managers and the buyer in the department store chain will be benefited through higher profits, but that the customers in the inner city may purchase an unwholesome food product and that their rights to proper products and personal respect will be ignored?

6. What are the economic outcomes?

   This shipment of a defective food product to an inner city community would result in economic efficiency only if the customers in that inner city community were fully informed. That clear is not the case

7. What are the legal requirements?

   I assume that it is against the law to knowingly sell a defective food product; it certainly would not get through the "Social Contract" or "Veil of Ignorance" tests of the legitimacy of a law.

8. What are the moral duties

Personal virtues. It would be impossible to be open, honest, truthful and proud of this proposed transaction.

Religious injunctions. This proposed transaction is not compassionate and kind, and it certainly does not create a sense of community between the inner city residents and the owners/managers of the department store.

Utilitarian benefits. The only social benefits are the very marginal increases in profits for the department store owners, managers and buyers; the social harms go beyond the financial losses of the customers, and would have to include monetary equivalents for their anger and disappointment.

Universal duties. The owners, managers and buyers of the department store chain would not want defective food products offer for sale unknowingly to them.

Distributive justice. The least among us in this instance are the inner city customers and residents, who certainly are being harmed.

Contributive liberty. No one's ability to develop their skills to the fullest seem to be affected by this unappetizing but non-health affecting action.

It seems fairly obvious that the practice of shipping defective goods to the ghetto was fairly common at the department store chain where Sara worked. Her mentor (Maria) knew the name and telephone number of the store in that lower income area without hesitation. Perhaps that is acceptable with fashions (dresses and other wearing apparel), textiles (sheets, towels, etc) or house wares (cups, plates and cooking utensils), but food products seem to cross over the boundary of what is permissible.

What happened? Sarah refused to ship the wafers, and was publicly derided for that action by Maria who called her "Saint Sarah" in front all the other buyers. When Sarah was unable to find another buyer to request her as an assistant at the next stage in the training program she was fired by the director of human resources who said that retailing required a "team approach", and that Sarah was obviously not a "team player". He refused to listen to her allegations about being asked to ship defective food products to unsuspecting customers, saying that Maria was a valued employee, that her decisions would have been in the best interest s of the firm, and that her instructions should have been followed. The president of the company refused to meet with Sarah, despite her sitting outside his office waiting for an opportunity for five days. The corporate attorney did come to see her there, explained that she had no evidence to support her claim, and that she would be forcefully removed if she remained on company property.

This is one of the few cases on business ethics where I love to explain the final end result. Sarah was not powerless. Her father was a senior partner in one of the largest law firms in San Francisco. Sarah enlisted his support. He said, "So they claim we have no evidence to support your claim, do they!", and sent agents into the convenience stores in southern California to purchase all of the cookies, still wrapped in their distinctive foil packaging, that they could find. Those purchases were videotaped, to prove the source. He then subpoenaed the records of the convenience store chain to establish that the wafers had come from the department store for which Sarah had worked.

Her father then hired an engineer to develop a method to determine which packages were infested. This could be done by using very sensitive microphones to listen to the sounds of the insects moving about within the packages. When he felt fully prepared he asked members of the board of directors of the department store chain to meet with him, saying that they could either meet privately with him in the board room or publicly in a court room.

At that meeting Sarah recounted her story, her father display the evidence he had gathered, and they then asked a member of the board to open one of the packages displayed upon the table. It was filled with insects, and everyone jumped back, away from the table. Sarah's father then said, "The next package that is opened with be opened in court, in front of a jury, unless you agree now, this afternoon, to our terms. Those terms included the firing of the president, the corporate attorney and the director human resources – all of whom had been involved in the firing of Sarah – and the donation of a substantial amount of money to charities located in the inner city neighborhoods in Southern California where the wafers have been sent for sale. The board accepted those terms. Sarah, rather than looking for another job in retailing, went to Law School.

Johnson Controls and Gender Equality

The company has been told, by the Supreme Court, that they can no longer continue to exclude women of child bearing age from high paying jobs in the production of lead-acid batteries. Most of the actual assembly work in this production process has been automated in recent years, and consequently most of the employment opportunities are in quality control, machine maintenance and laboratory analysis tasks. But, all of these activities involve being physically present on the factory floor and consequently result in some exposure to the harmful effects of lead. Lead is a heavy metal that can have exceedingly harmful effects upon the fetus if absorbed into the mother's body even in very minimal amounts prior to or during pregnancy.

This case is complicated because there is no single existing or planned company action to evaluate. Instead, there are three. The company has been told that they cannot continue their existing action, but they have developed three planned alternatives: 1) stop operations in the U.S. and move all production overseas; 2) continue operations as is in the U.S. with women in the high paying and high risk jobs and essentially hope for the best; or 3) continue operations in the U.S., but with greatly heightened safety standards that it was expected would deal with the basic problem of possible danger to the fetus. . I frequently assign groups to make presentations in support of each alternative, with the balance of the class being divided into six to eight member boards of directors who must make the final decision.

For the purposes of this teaching note I will evaluate the first "move overseas" alternative. Clearly the benefits and harms, the rights recognized and the rights denied, will differ for the other two, but I assume that those differences will be clear:

1. What groups will be benefited if all battery production is moved overseas?

    Company owners and managers will benefit from increased profits (case says up 25%
    due to lower wage rates) and decreased probability of law suits
    Foreign workers will benefit from existence of skilled jobs; company could probably in-
    sist upon all male work force in most 3rd world countries.
    Children of domestic workers will not be exposed to toxic effects of lead

2. What groups will be harmed if all battery production is moved overseas

    Domestic workers will be harmed by the export of skilled and high paying jobs
    Foreign workers, even if all male, may be harmed by lead exposure
    Children of foreign workers, if not all male, may be harmed by lead exposure

3. What groups will be able to exercise their rights by moving all battery production overseas?

    Company owners and managers have a right to decide on lcgal place of production
    Children of domestic workers have a right to a healthy life

4. What groups will be unable to exercise their rights if production is moved overseas

    Domestic employees who did not file the "equal rights" law suit have a right to high pay-
    ing jobs; certainly they did nothing to force the company to move overseas.
    Foreign workers have a right to a healthy work environment
    Children of foreign workers have a right to a healthy life

5. Express the moral problems so that everyone involved will believe that their particular inter-
    ests (both outcomes and rights) have been included and considered:

    Is it "right" that Johnson Controls mover all lead-acid batter production overseas, given
    that the owners/managers will benefit from higher profits and lesser likelihood of law
    suits, but also given that domestic workers will be harmed by the loss of their jobs and
    that foreign workers may be harmed by the exposure to lead. The owners/managers have
    a right to decide o the proper place of production, but the domestic workers who were not
    involved in the original law suit have a right to continued employment and the foreign
    workers who will be hired have a right to health for themselves and their children

6. What are the economic benefits?

    There certainly are factor markets for labor that set the wages in 3rd world countries, and
    there is no question but that those markets are very competitive, but the participants – the
    workers selling their time – probably are not informed of the dangers in this instance.

7. What are the legal requirements?

It can be assumed that the governments in 3rd world countries do not have stringent workplace laws governing the level of exposure to lead.

8. What are the ethical duties?

Personal virtues. I would assume that the company would not be open, honest and truthful about the dangers of exposure to lead while they were recruiting women workers overseas, and it would be hard to be proud of the possible effects.

Religious injunctions. The use of foreign workers to perform a potentially dangerous job would not be kind and compassionate, and would not create a sense of community, of everyone working together for a common goal.

Utilitarian benefits. The net social benefits here would depend upon the negative values that were computed for the possible health effects from lead exposure to the workers overseas and to their children

Universal duties. The owners and managers of the firm would not wish to work in an environment that could be hazardous to their health

Distributive justice. Clearly the people overseas who were recruited for these jobs constitute the "least among us", and they may well be harmed.

Contributive liberty. Equally clearly the people overseas who accept these jobs and there are harmed by the lead exposure will be unable to develop their skills to the fullest.

If you assign three groups to make presentations to the balance of the class, whom you then divide into six to eight person "boards of directors" and give perhaps 10 minutes to meet and reach a decision, you will find that the "propose convincing moral solution" outcome of the moral reasoning process (Figure 1 in Chapter I) is amply demonstrated. The argument in support of the 3rd alternative – continue to operate all three plants at their present domestic locations, but with greatly heightened safety standards – are overwhelming. Look at the following listing of the ethical principles in favor of this choice:

Personal virtues. Company executives can be open, honest and truthful about the workplace conditions of this alternative, and they can be proud also.

Religious injunctions. This action can be considered to be kind and compassionate, and ought to provide managers and workers with a sense of community and common purpose.

Utilitarian benefits. Here the net social benefits will depend upon the positive values placed upon the health benefits to workers and their children.

Universal duties. The owners and managers of the firm would, I would assume, be willing to work in a potentially hazardous job given the highest possible safety standards.

Distributive justice. I would assume that the domestic workers and their children would be the "least among us" in this situation, and they are not to be harmed. .

Contributive liberty. It would seem that the domestic workers and their children, given the greatly heightened safety standards, would be to to develop their skills to the fullest.

What happened? I don't know. I hope that the company was able to negotiate some wage reductions and was willing to absorb the balance of the costs needed to continue the automated production of lead-acid batteries in this country. The automation of low paying jobs, and the consequent generation of high paying jobs in machine repair, quality control and computer programming, appeals to me as a proper reaction to the drive to reduce costs and improve productivity, but I'm not certain that happened. I called the public relations officer at Johnson Controls a couple of times, but was unable to reach that person and he/she never returned my calls. Unfortunately, to me, that indicates that they probably moved the battery manufacturing operations overseas.

H. B. Fuller and the Sale of Resistol

This, as I explained in the suggested syllabus given in the "Introduction" section of this teacher's guide, is a great case, written by Norman Bowie and Stefanie Lenway, both of the Carlson School of Management at the University of Minnesota. It is complex because, as with the Johnson Controls case discussed just previously, there are a number of alternatives, and not just "sell the product" or "don't sell the product" choices. Let me start this teaching note by listing those alternatives, together with the major drawbacks associated with each:

Continue sales of unaltered Resistol. The problem here is that this will continue to harm the street children of the region, and the adults who have to either tolerate or deal with those street children. This is by far the most profitable of all the choices

Continue sales of Resistol, but add oil of mustard. This seems like a "natural", but it will harm the legitimate users of the product (who will have to breath the fumes in unventilated buildings) and doubtless will decrease sales (unless all competitors act jointly)

Continue sales of Resistol, but change the solvent. The case says that this will be very difficult, and I assume that is true. The molecular structure of any volatile (quick drying) solvent is just automatically going to have hallucinogenic properties in the fumes.

Continue sales of Resistol, but donate substantial social help. The idea here is to attempt to deal directly with the problem, which is the deprived existence of the street children. It would be possible, but expensive, to support orphanages and schools

Continue industrial sales but restrict consumer sales. The proposal here is to sell the un-altered product only to industrial suppliers, but the case says that this will not limit access to the street vendors who either buy it or steal it from those suppliers.

Stop all sales, but offer water-based substitutes that require either micro-wave or infra-red dryers. The case says that the small manufacturers are not able to afford the indus-trial dryers, and the electrical distribution system can't support them.

Stop all sales, and get out of the quick-setting adhesive business in Latin America. The case says that this will affect the paint sales for most industrial suppliers in the area only hand one brand of paints and adhesives.

I often assign three groups to make three different presentations to the balance of the class. I divide the balance of the class into six to eight person boards of directors who, after lis-tening to those presentations, meet for 10 minutes, and decide what H. B. Fuller should do. The three groups that make presentations have to meet before the class, and put together those presentations either on Power Point or on vue-graph slides. The three alternatives that those small groups (generally 3 persons per group) are told to prepare and then present are listed below. I think that these are the technically and economically viable ones:

Continue sales of unaltered Resistol. This group is to make the argument, expressed in the case by Humberto Larach, that this addiction is a problem of the society, not of the company. It is unfortunate what happens to the children, he insisted, but it is their choice to misuse this product, and the overall benefits to the small manufacturers and household users outweigh those harms.

Continue sales of Resistol but altered by the addition of the oil of mustard. This group is to make the argument that the harms to the addicted children outweigh the benefits to the legitimate users, and that the company has to take some action. They will have to recog-nize the harms to the workers at the small manufacturers, unless ventilation is improved, and try to counter the potential lose of sales by advertising a "community" effort

Continue sales of Resistol, but make a concerted effort to deal with the real problem, which is the addiction of the deprived street children. Sales of Resistol in Central Ameri-can in the case are estimated to be $12 million; profits are not given but 10% or $1.2 mil-lion would not be unlikely. This group should argue for an expenditure of $500,000 for orphanages and schools, and a campaign to get "community" support and effort.

The following outline is based upon the "continue the sale of Resistol, unaltered" alterna-tive. The distribution of benefits and harms, the exercise and denial of rights, and the conclu-sions from economics, law and ethics, would of course differ for the other two.

1. What groups will be benefited from continuing the sale of the unaltered adhesive?

   Owners and managers of H. B. Fuller, who will continue to gain profits.

Legitimate users (small factories and repair shops) in Central America, who find the product ideal for their needs
Legitimate distributors in Central America, who provide a useful service

2. What groups will be harmed by continuing the sale of the unaltered adhesive?

Street children (homeless and poor), who will continue to misuse the product
Citizens of Central America who must deal with the problem

3. What groups will be able to exercise their rights through the continued sale

Owners and managers of H.B. Fuller have a right to sell a legitimate product, but this product is no longer legal in one part of the region due to recent action by legislature Honduras mandating use of oil of mustard
Legitimate users in Central America who have a right to conduct their businesses their ways, but again the adhesive is now illegal in part of the region

4. What groups will be unable to exercise their rights if the sales continue?

Street children have a right to health, but they are the ones making the choice to abuse the adhesive.
Citizens of the region have a right to have their laws obeyed. Humberto Larach, of H. B. Fuller, believes that the law mandating oil of mustard will not be enforced, and consequently need not be obeyed. The does contradict the rights of the citizens

5. Express the moral problem so that everyone will believe that their interests have been recognized and included:

Is it "right" that H. B. Fuiller continue the sale of the unaltered adhesive given that this is a very useful product for the small factories and repair shops of Central America, and a very profitable one for H. B. Fuller, but also given that its misuse by the street children of that region in ruining their lives and creating a large problem for the society of the region? H. B. Fuller clearly has a right to sell a legal product, but that legality is now in question due to an unenforced law, and the street children clearly have a right to health, but that right is also in question as they are the ones making the choice to abuse their own health.

6. What are the economic benefits?

Resistol is a very useful product, given the stage of industrial development in the region. There is an established market, and legitimate demand, for the unaltereddhesive, and those customers must be informed about both the properties and effects of the adhesive; it would be impossible for someone living in the region to remain ignorant of the addicted children. However, those children represent an external cost imposed upon the society

7. What are the legal requirements?

> There is a law in Honduras mandating the use of oil of mustard in all quick setting adhesives, but it is probable that the law will not be enforced. The question then becomes whether a law that is not or cannot be enforced is truly a "law". Chapter III states that a law has to be consistent, universal, published, accepted and enforced. The last two conditions appear to be missing here.

8. What are the ethical principles?

> Personal virtues. The company can be open, honest and truthful about continuing the sales of the unaltered adhesive, but it is questionable if they can be proud.

> Religious injunctions. The continued sale cannot be considered to be kind and compassionate to the children, and does not bring everyone together to address this problem

> Utilitarian benefits. The social benefits of the continued use of the unaltered adhesive by the small factories and shops are undeniable; the social costs of addicted children are hard to estimate.

> Universal duties. Would the executives of H.B. Fuller want a Central American company to sell a product in the United States that was addictive to their children?

> Distributive justice. There would appear to be no question but that the street children in Central America are the "least among us". They are being hurt.

> Contributive liberty. This seems to be a wash. The ability of the street children to develop their skills to the fullest is being denied by the continued sale of the unaltered adhesive, but those same abilities will be denied to the legitimate users if the product is make unavailable or altered so as to become nearly unusable.

> What happened? H. B. Fuller made a public statement that they would withdraw Resistol from the market, but then evidently changed their mind (or intended their announcement to apply only to the retail sector) for Resistol has continued to be sold for industrial use in Central America.

<u>Teaching Notes for Chapter IV – Moral Analysis and Ethical Duties</u>

The basic argument of this chapter is that moral philosophy adds one more evaluative dimension, or moral perspective, to help in making decisions that result in positive outcomes and the recognition of rights for some and negative results and the denial of rights for others, Philosophy, of course, is the study of thought and conduct and moral philosophy is the study of proper thought and conduct; that is, how we should think and ought to behave. Essentially moral philosophy proposes the existence of a set of objective norms of behavior and universal statements of belief that are "right", "just" and "fair" in, of and by themselves. The norms and beliefs that all of us hold intuitively are based upon our religious and cultural traditions and our economic and social situations. They are subjective and personal; they vary between people. But there are some norms and beliefs that can be said to be objective and universal, to be based upon reason rather than emotion. These can be considered to be "right" and "just" and "fair" in, of and by themselves because they can be logically seen to lead to a "good" society in which everyone will have equal degrees of liberty, opportunity, dignity and respect. This is "moral reasoning", logically working from an objective and universal first principle through to a decision on the ethical duties we owe to others. There are some problems here also; though perhaps not as serious as in the other two approaches of economic efficiency and legal obedience. Moral reasoning does recognize the nature and value the worth of individual human beings as expressed by their needs for liberty, opportunity, dignity and respect.

The chapter discusses six of those objective norms of behavior or universal statements of belief that can be considered to be based upon reason rather than emotion, and that can be said to lead to a good society n which everyone will have equal degrees of liberty, opportunity, dignity and respect. Those objective norms or universal statements are 1) Eternal Law; 2) Personal Virtue; 3) Utilitarian Benefit; 4)Universal Duties; 5) Distributive Justice and 6) Contributive Liberty. The problem is to get students to use, and so become familiar with, those six concepts. Market forces and legal requirements are familiar ideas (or ideals) to most members of my classes; ethical principles are not familiar, and I find that students have to be encouraged to use them. The greatest fear most of my students seem to have is that of being laughed at by their peers, of being derided for an excess of social consciousness. I try to be as supportive as possible, and often announce that no one in the class will ever be on their own in making an honest attempt to apply moral reasoning to managerial problems. I will always try to help. Now, on to the assignment questions, the class start-ups, and the different cases:

1. Assignment questions. Normally I don't, as I have explained numerous times in the past in these notes, use assignment questions as a means of introducing concepts to students because I think that they are largely ignored in the students' preparation. This chapter on ethical duties might well be an exception because truly thought provoking questions are possible, and do seem to get students more comfortable with these important concepts. Here are some assignment questions I have used in the past:

   Moral standards of behavior are said to be subjective and personal. Ethical principles of analysis are said to be objective and universal. What makes them objective and universal, and why is that important?

Why does the Golden Rule appear in almost all of the world's religions? Is it because this concept has been verbally transmitted from one religion to the next, or does it represent some basic feature in the human character?

The ancient Greek philosophers believed that the goal of human existence was the "active, rational pursuit of excellence". Do you accept that as the goal of human existence? If not, what in your view should be the goal of human existence?

The Utilitarian principle claims that we should always select the alternative with the greatest net social benefit (excess of good over harm). That seems simple, but in reality it is complex. What makes it complex?

If you were asked to defend the ethical principle that we should never harm the least amongst us, those with least income, education and power to influence events, how would you do so. Why should people accept that as an objective and universal rule of conduct?

2. Start-up suggestions. I also, as explained earlier, generally move directly to the discussion of the cases rather than review the content of the reading. I find that if I force students to use the concepts from each of the chapters they will learn those concepts better than if we discuss them in detail. This seems to me to be particularly true in the early stages of the course when I want to get the students to feel more comfortable talking about their opinions, their views, their beliefs and their values. By the time we get to Chapter IV on ethical duties members of my classes do appear to feel more comfortable in those areas, but now they are uncomfortable in talking about objective norms and universal beliefs. It does, however, break up the routine to start talking about concepts from the readings and/or issues from the newspapers.

If you want to try some issues taken from the newspapers let me suggest that privacy in employment always seems to be thought provoking. Should an employer read employee e-mails sent and received over office computers during normal work hours? Should an employer videotape employee actions in offices, hallways, factories and lounges (though not restrooms)? If, like me, you prefer to get right to the cases, then here are my notes on the three that follow Chapter IV.

Good Life at RJR Nabisco

I must admit that I like the two sequential cases that focus on RJR Nabisco. They are both – in my view – outrageous in their executive self-centeredness, but the actions in each are at least partially market driven and so can be classified as economically efficient, and they also fit generally, though not precisely, within the law. To condemn those actions members of my classes are forced to rely on such ethical concepts as Personal Virtue and Distributive Justice and familiarity with the use of those concepts is, of course, the goal of this series of classes.

The "Good Life at RJR Nabisco" describes a situation in which the senior executives are very well paid, receive what certainly appear to be envious perks, and live a very lavish life style. That life style is perhaps best epitomized by the description in the case of the RJR Nabisco hanger at the Atlanta airport. I often read this short paragraph to the class, and ask, "Has any one been in a aircraft hanger like this? What does the typical aircraft hanger look like?

The RJR Nabisco jet hangar was not a sheet metal building of the type that is commonly seen at airports. Instead, it was a three-story building of tinted glass, surrounded by $250,000 in landscaping. A visitor entered through a tall open "atrium", with a roof made of glass panels, floors laid in Italian marble, and walls paneled with Dominican mahogany. $600,000 in furniture was spread trough the pilots' lounge and the control, which were also decorated with 4100,000 in paintings and statuary.

The high salaries, abundant perks and lavish life styles could be considered to be harmless if the senior executives were focused on improving the long-term performance of the firm and creating outstanding value for the shareholders, if those salaries, perks and life styles were rewards for having created that value for the shareholders In the first "Good Life" case it is not altogether clear that is not has occurred. Senior executives at many companies are very well paid and receive enviable benefits. It is possible to claim that those are simply the market driven costs of hiring and retaining highly qualified senior people, and that RJR Nabisco happens to have hired and wants to retain exceptionally qualified senior people. That claim is overridden by the events in the second "Leveraged Buyout" case in which it is clear that there is an awful lot of money being wasted or the price for the buyout, which presumably would impose much stricter controls, would not be so high. I usually take up both cases on the same day, and break up the class into groups who are assigned one of those cases (usually "Good Life' for the front half of the room; "Leveraged Buyout" for the back half). Those groups meet for about 20 minutes during class time, and come back to report to the balance of the class on whether they think that the situation described in "their" case is "right" or not. I assume that by this stage in the course those groups use the standard analytical format of this course more or less automatically: I expect them to summarize that analytical format upon a vue-graph slide.

1. What groups are benefited by the corporate expenditures to support the senior executives?

   Corporate executives, with high salaries, luxury cars and numerous club memberships
   Sports figures, with large payments and little work
   Pilots (and some other employees), with luxurious workplaces and also little work
   Company owners, if executive perks truly do motivate superior performance

2. What groups are harmed by the corporate expenditures to support the senior executives?

   Stockholders, unless salaries and perks truly do motivate effort and improve performance
   Employees, who seem to be left out of the life style, and may be harmed by a declining competitive posture of the company if the salaries and perks do not motivate performance
   Customers, who have to pay for the life style in higher margins on their purchases

3. What groups are able to fully exercise their rights if the present payments continue?

   Corporate executives have a right to be paid market wages; the question is whether these are at "market" or "far above market" levels

4. What groups will be denied some of their rights if the present payments continue?

    Stockholders; it can be argued that they have a right to know about the extent of these payments and perks?
    Employees; it can be argued that their jobs are being put at risk.

5. Express the moral problem so that everyone involved will believe that their particular interests have been recognized and included

    Is it right that RJR Nabisco continue to support the high salaries, numerous perks and luxurious lifestyles of the senior executives, given that this may motivate those executive to superior performance, or may simply be a waste of stockholder funds and a detraction from manage attention?

6. What are the economic benefits?

    The economic argument in favor of continuing the current level of payments is that of incentives payment. Managers and others work to get what they want, and they work hardest to get what they want most. All of us may not want an aircraft hanger with Italian marble floors and Dominican mahogany walls, but if that is what drives Ross Johnson and his coterie to improved performance, then who are we to object?

7. What are the legal requirements?

    There is no law against paying high salaries and awarding large perks. Those salaries and perks have to be approved by the Board of Directors, but in this case the Board seems to consist of friends of Ross Johnson. The company is not breaking the law as currently written, and may not be breaking the law as thoughtfully derived from a Social Contract or Veil of Ignorance process.

8. What are the ethical duties?

    Personal virtues. The action is not "open, truthful and honest" in that the stockholders have not been told of the high payments. It is doubtful if the senior executives are "boastfully proud" of their largesse.

    Religious injunctions. The action is neither kind nor unkind, compassionate nor uncompassionate; it merely seems to be selfish. However, selfish actions do not bring everyone together in pursuit of a common goal.

    Utilitarian benefits. It is hard to determine if these large payments create a net social benefit because the motivational effects are not known.

    Universal duties. It is hard to determine if these large payments should be univeralized (right for everyone) because the harmful consequences are not known

Distributive justice. It is hard to determine if these large payments harm the "least amongst us" because, once again, the motivational effects are not known.

Contributive liberty. it is hard, lastly, to determine if these large payments will interfere with anyone's right to self-development because, once more, the final consequences are not known.

My students usually conclude that "everyone does it" (meaning every company makes large payments and provides large perks to senior executives). I try, usually unsuccessfully, to explain that just because "everyone does it" does not necessarily make it "right". I try to explain, generally with greater success, that the reason they find it so difficult to evaluate those payments, perks and life styles is that the motivational effects and future consequences are not known with certainty. When that conclusion seems to be at least partially accepted, we move on to the second case:

Leveraged Buyout of RJR Nabisco

Again, this is one of my favorite cases. The amounts of money are huge. The failures of responsibility are extreme. And, it fits so neatly with the earlier "Good Life" case where the consequences of the high salaries, large perks and luxurious life styles were not clear. Now those outcomes are very clear for the control of RJR Nabisco would not command such a large premium over market price were not cost reductions and revenue enhancements so apparently possible. In short, the senior management was not doing its job

Ross Johnson, saying that he had been disappointed at his lack of success in raising the stock price for RJR Nabisco, the tobacco/food products conglomerate he had headed for a number of years, offered to "take the company private {that is, buy a controlling interest in the company). The stock at the time of his offer was selling at $56 per share. He offered to purchase the controlling interest at $75 per share; his argument was that the market, as presented by analysts at Wall Street firms, had misevaluated the potential growth of the firm. Mr. Johnson said that he wanted to "increase value for the shareholders".

Mr. Johnson's offer at $75 per share was quickly followed by an offer from a private investment bank and "buyout" specialist (Kohlberg, Kravis Roberts) at $90 per share. Mr. Johnson countered with an offer at $92.00 per share, and said that the buyout specialist wanted to break up the company and sell off the pieces while he, Mr. Johnson, would keep the company together and preserve jobs, etc. Kohlberg Kravis then leaked a mem of understanding between Mr. Johnson and the investment bank supporting his offer that detailed similar plans to break up the firm and payments in the form of stock to Mr. Johnson and six to nine other RJR Nabisco in the amount of $1.87 to $4.40 billion in return for an investment of only $20 million, and that to be in the form of an interest-free loan from the company. Eventually Mr. Johnson and Shearson Lehman Brothers won the control of RJR Nabisco with a bid of $114 per share. I start the discussion of this case by making certain that members of the class understand the benefits and harms of the proposed buyout:

1. What groups will be benefited by the leveraged buyout as proposed at the end of the case?

Investor group members (Ross Johnson and Shearson Lehman)	$11,200 million
Company stockholders (amount above prior market value)	12,150 million
Investment banks (fees for advice & commissions for bonds)	400 million
Law firms (fees for advice and drafting of documents)	250 million
Commercial banks (fees for the commitment of loans)	175 million
Total	$24,175 million

2. What groups will be harmed by the leveraged buyout as proposed at the end of the case?

Government tax losses (interest on the debt exempted from taxes)	$5,000 million
Existing bondholder losses (bond values decline with more debt)	520 million
24,200 employees discharged to save money to repay debt)	not estimated
Total	5,520 million

3. What groups will be able to fully exercise their rights if the leveraged buyout continues?

Ross Morgan and other senior executive have a right to determine what they believe to be in the best interests of the company stockholders
Company stockholders have a right to determine what they believe to be in their best interests
Investment banks, law firms and commercial banks have a right to sell their advice and services

4. What groups will be denied some of their rights if the leveraged buyout continues

Existing bondholders have a right to have the value of their original investments maintained
Existing employees may have a right to have their original employment contracts maintained. They are being fired not to improve the performance of the company, but to generate greater profits for an investor group

5. Express the moral problem so that everyone involved will believe that their particular interests have been recognized and included

Is it right that Ross Johnson and Shearson Lehman Brothers arranged a leveraged buyout of RJR Nabisco, given that there will be immediate returns to the investor group, existing stockholders and advisory firms but also given that there will be financial losses to existing bondholders and job losses to existing employees?

6. What are the economic benefits?

There is no question but that there is a free and competitive market for the stock of RJR Nabisco, and Ross Johnson and Shearson Lehman Brothers are willing to purchase the stock at a premium on that market from willing sellers. It is also clear the Ross Johnson plans to take action to increase the efficiency of RJR Nabisco by reducing the high salaries, perks and life styles and by demanding greater effort from all surviving employees. One question, from the economic perspective, is whether Ross Johnson had a duty to the original stockholders to take exactly those actions which would have raised the stock price without the need for a leveraged buyout. Another question, also from the economic perspective, is whether the external costs to be imposed upon the original bondholders and the original employees have been included in the computations.

7. What are the legal requirements.

There certainly is no law against leveraged buyouts. The question is whether people who did not know what position they would hold – member of the investment group, existing stockholder, current bondholder, current employee, or just casual observer – decide should be the law on leveraged buyouts.

8. What are the ethical duties?

Personal virtues. The first proposal for the leveraged buyout was not open, honest and truthful. It id not disclose the ownership positions of Ross Johnson and his senior associates, not was it truthful about his intent to sell off many successful portions of the firm

Religious injunctions. The leveraged buyout was kind and compassionate, and did not bring everyone – investment groups, advisory firms existing stockholders, current bondholder and current employees – together with a sense of community and a common goal.

Utilitarian benefits. It does appear that the benefits ($24.2 billion) will be greater than the harms ($5.5 billion plus the loss of 24,000 jobs). Of course, that depends on the value placed on the lost jobs, but that value would have to be very high to sway the outcome.

Universal duties. If it is right for the investor group to take money from the current bondholders and jobs from the current employees, then it has to be right for other to do that to the investor group. That does seem accepted in the world high finance.

Distributive justice. The least among us in this instance are doubtless the people who will lose their jobs.

Contributive liberty. It can also be claimed that the people who lost their jobs will not have an opportunity to develop their skills to the fullest.

What happened? As you doubtless know RJR Nabisco was purchased not by Ross Johnson and Shearson Lehman Brothers but by Kohlberg, Kravis Roberts. The board of directors of RJR Nabisco said that it was concerned by the self-serving nature of Ross Johnson's proposal; $4.40 billion in stock of the purchased company was to go a group of six to nine senior executives, including Johnson, in return for an investment of $20 million that came from an interest free loan from the company. They also said that they were concerned by the lack of truthfulness in many of the statements by Ross Johnson relative to the break-up of the company. They accepted the lower bid, at $109 per share, from Kohlberg, Kravis Roberts. The leveraged buyout did not "work", however. Evidently they paid too much for the company, and it took many years, and many sacrifices by uninvolved persons, to finally achieve a breakeven status.

WalMart and Expansion into Smaller Towns

I suggest that you start the class discussion by reading the first paragraph in the in the class assignment:

> You are the Michigan district manager for WalMart. Petoskey is one of the few remaining "untapped" areas in the state; the nearest Wal-Mart stores are 45 to 60 miles away, at Gaylord to the east and Mackinac City to the north. At both locations store closings and the decay of the central business district did follow the introduction of the discount chain; neither, however, is a tourist destination so that the impact upon tourism can't really be measured and then applied to Petoskey. You have just received the appeal, signed by 22,000 people, saying "Please don't destroy our town; we love it just the way it is." What do you do, and why?

You always have your choice, in these case discussion, of just asking for the actions that the students would take and hoping that an underlying structure will appear as students propose alternatives and question facts, or of imposing a structure so that all of the facts and alternatives are listed, and then asking for opinions. I try to vary the class discussions between those two modes, to maintain interest, but it is much easier to write a useful teaching note for the imposed structure

1. Who will be benefited by the new store and mall in Petoskey?

   WalMart stockholders, who will gain from higher profits
   WalMart managers, who will benefit from increased sales and bonuses
   Local customers, who will benefit from lower prices and wider selections

2. Who will be harmed by the new store and mall in Petoskey?

   Local merchants, who will lose business and probably close as unable to compete
   Vacation visitors, who will lose the ambiance as the attractive downtown deteriorates
   Summer residents, who will also lose ambiance and watch the town's character change
   All residents, who will have to make up 20% to 25% shortfall in taxes
   All residents will have 20% to 25% fewer jobs available

3. Whose rights will be exercised, and made more certain?

   WalMart managers, who have a right to expand their business legally
   Local customers who have a right to competitive markets

4. Whose rights will be denied or ignored if the new store and mall are built?

   Local residents have a right to majority rule
   Local residents have a right to have laws obeyied

5. State the moral problem so that all sides will believe their interests have been recognized:

   Is it "right" that WalMart open a new, very large and very efficient store and mall in Pe-toskey, given that this will increase profits and better serve customers, but also given that it will result in fewer jobs and higher taxes for the residents, probably change the appeal-ing character of the historic downtown, and is technically illegal.

6. If we look at this problem from the viewpoint of economic theory, what are the conclusions?

   WalMart managers are responding to a market demand that they have not manipulated in any way. There are customers in the area who truly want the lower prices and wider se-lections that WalMart does offer, and those customers are fully informed. WalMart man-gers have no obligations to their competitors, the downtown merchants who will find it difficult to offer comparative prices and products. The only economic problems are the external costs that the company will be imposing on the community in the form of the de-terioration they are bringing to the downtown, and in the form of the changed tax burden they are imposing upon the homeowners.

7. If we look at this problem from the viewpoint of legal theory, what are the conclusions?

   Legal theory would also seem clear, at least on the surface. It is certainly lawful for a company to enter a new market, despite the consequences of that entrance upon existing competitors. But, the land WalMart has selected for the new store and mall is not zoned for commercial development, and the company will need to "use large numbers of corpo-rate attorneys in continuous hearings, suits, and appeals to simply override opposition" Overriding opposition through the use of economic power is not the true meaning of the Social Contract concept

8. If we look at the problem from the point of view of moral theory, what are the conclusions?

   Personal virtues. The company has been open, honest and truthful about their intentions, and assumably they are proud of their low prices and wide selections.

   Religious injunctions. The new stores is not going to form a sense of community, of eve-ryone working for a common goal. Instead it will divide summer residents and vacation visitors even more from the year round residents who appear in large measure to want the store.

Utilitarian benefits. It would seem that the new store will create great net benefits than harms for all of the people in Petoskey, though that will depend upon the value that is placed on the lost historical character and appeal of the downtown and harbor.

Universal duties. Would the senior executives at WalMart want a similar store placed in the towns where they live? WalMart does have a different corporate culture from most other very large and very successful American corporations, and the answer probably is "yes".

Distributive justice. It is hard to classify the summer residents and vacation visitors as the "least amongst us" in this situation, and they are in large measure the ones who will be harmed. Working people within the area will be benefited

Contributive liberty. It is also hard to say that anyone's right to develop their skills to the fullest will be harmed by the new WalMart store and mall in Petoskey.

There were a number of alternatives that were mentioned in the case, but most of those seem not to be fully viable. The case says that the 67 acre site that WalMart owns is one of the few local areas that is level enough for commercial development. Doubtless there are other level sites in Emmet County, but the case also says that Petoskey is the trading center for the region; the further away the store is placed the less business it might be expected to attract. People will drive a considerable distance to get to a WalMart, but there are limits, especially in northern Michigan where lake-effect snow will be a problem through the winter. A smaller version of the mall, or a smaller version of the store, perhaps in an older factory building, would certainly reduce opposition and limit damages to the downtown harbor area, but those less obtrusive versions also may attract much less business. It is necessary to remember that the "high volume/low cost" strategy was what made WalMart successful in the past, and the district manager probably wants to continue those proven policies. I have had students recommend that WalMart subsidize the downtown merchants, or make up for the lost tax revenues with special payments to the city, but those philanthropic policies might be difficult for a district manager to initiate.

There are also a number of issues or outcomes that are not certain. For example, I think that it is fairly clear that in most small towns many of the downtown family-owned businesses that offer competing products in men's women's or children's clothing, housewares, paints and hardware products, sporting goods, automotive parts, electronic appliances and drug, cosmetic and health care products are forced to close when MalMart enters the area. They simply can't compete against WalMart's huge economics of scale. But, Petoskey is not your typical small town; it has the advantage of summer residents and vacation tourists, both of whom may fit in a market segment and income classification that seldom shops at MalMart.

What happened? The large WalMart store and mall were built on the land owned by WalMart on the southern edge of Petoskey despite the energetic opposition of many in the community. WalMart executives claim that this new location has been very successful, and in 1999 they substantially enlarged the store. Summer residents continue to boycott it, and say that the visible business at that store is far less than at other WalMart locations. Many of the downtown stores have closed, and there is now a very decided "boarded up" appearance to the harbor area.

Teaching Notes for Chapter V – Why Should a Business Manager Be Moral?

I really like this chapter. The basic message is that there are three different reasons for a manager to attempt to be moral in his or her decisions and actions that affect other people, and to attempt to logically convince those people that he or she has been moral in those decisions and action. The first reason, of course, is reciprocity. If we don't worry about the "rightness", "justness" and "fairness" of our actions towards others, then we cannot really expect others to be worried about the "rightness", "justness" and "fairness" of their actions towards us. That is not compelling to many people, however. As the text explains the world is filled with people who will say, "We're going to try to get what we want right now, and we'll worry about your treatment of us latter on and, if we do get what we want right now we won't have to worry about your treatment of us latter on because we will have moved beyond your ability to retaliate".

The second reason to be moral is much stronger. It is a concern for the quality of our lives, for the dignity of our goals and the standards by which we live. I think that the most basic question in ethics is "Do we have an obligation to leave the world a little better than we found it, or can we simply take what we want now, and leave it to others to worry about making up for any shortfall later one?" I think that many people do recognize this obligation, though they may never have sorted out that general duty into specific responsibilities to their professions, their organizations, their communities, and their careers. But, once again the world is filled with people who do not accept this "make the world a little better" duty, who focus much more on the material benefits that seem to be available to them today, and so once again perhaps we need something more than the quality of life as the reason to convince others to be moral.

The third reason to be moral is, in my view, the strongest of all. We should be moral because the success of our organization is dependent upon cooperative efforts by everyone associated with that organization. But, why should those people – the stakeholders who can affect the achievement of the organization's objectives – cooperate? These stakeholder constitute a wide range of persons: factory and office workers, functional and technical managers, senior executives, scientists and engineers, suppliers, distributors, customers, creditors, owners and local residents. Why should those people cooperate with us and – even more – why should they share their innovations with us? The first major argument of this chapter is that moral responsibility, moral reasoning and moral character in the modern "extended" organization lead to trust, commitment and effort:

Corporate mgt. in extended organizations	{	Recognition of moral responsibility -What is "duty"?	}	Trust
		Application of moral reasoning -What is "right"?		Commitment
		Possession of moral character -What is "integrity"?		Effort

Maybe the basic answer to the "Why be moral?" question is the need for a manager to build trust, commitment and effort among all of the individuals and groups associated with his or her organization. Maybe trust is the essential first step, and perhaps we can't get commitment and effort without that trust. And, maybe trust is built upon our making and explaining our decisions and actions in a way that most people –we can probably never convince all – can agree to be "right" and "just" and "fair". This is the first basic argument of Chapter V, that trust requires, a recognition of moral responsibility, an application of moral reasoning, and a possession of moral character or courage:

The second basic argument of Chapter V is that trust, commitment and effort, when supported by consistent managerial policies, lead to cooperation, innovation and – for want of a better term – unification, or the sense of everyone working jointly for a common goal. And, the third basic argument of Chapter V is that cooperation, innovation and that sense of everyone working jointly will lead– though there is not room to put this on the graphic –to competitive success and financial achievement:

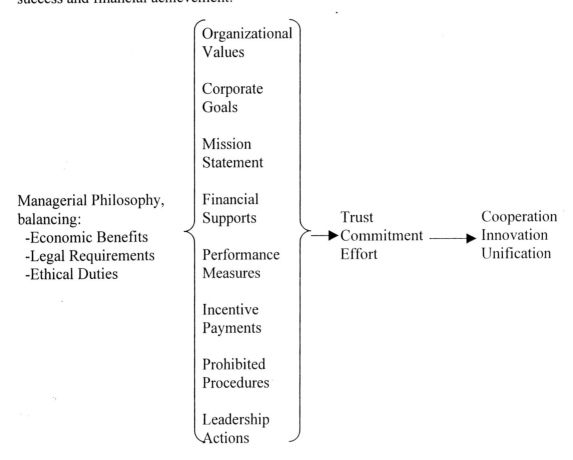

1. Assignment questions. For Chapter V I do use assignment questions, but they are very blunt and direct. I want members of my classes not to "buy into" these concepts – that takes time – but to consider them seriously. Consequently I challenge them:

   Do you believe that managers in a business firm are dependent upon the trust, commitment and effort of others?

If so, then how do you build that trust, commitment and effort and, particularly, how do you guide it towards a common goal?

Have you ever been a member of an organization that had a high degree of trust, commitment and effort, and that evidenced a large amount of cooperation, innovation and unification, a feeling that we're all working towards a common goal? If so, what was the cause, what – in your opinion – made all that happen?

Have you ever been a member of an organization that had a very low degree of trust, commitment and effort, and that evidenced a very small amount of cooperation, innovation and unification, where there was almost no feeling that everyone was working together for a common goal. If so, what was the cause here?

2. Start-up methods. The discussion at this stage of the course reflects the comfort level the students have developed – or have not developed -- in the earlier classes of the course. I start with the last question. Sometimes we get very lively description of the truly sad organizations in which some members of the class have worked, and the cause that is ascribed is almost always the alleged self-centeredness of the management. Students will often describe athletic teams as examples of organizations with high degrees of trust, commitment and effort, and here the alleged reason is that of the common goal. It does not happen often but occasionally a member of the class will have been part of an elite military unit – Army Ranger, Marine Corps, or Navy Seal –and will talk about the common goal and intensive training.

I move the class along to the discussion of the cases as soon as the interest in the assignment questions begins to slow down. As shown in the proposed outline of the course in the "General Suggestions for Teaching the Ethics of Management", the first section of this booklet, I assign Chapter V and all three cases on the same day: Class 11. I divide the class into thirds (right, center and left), and assign each of the cases to one of those sections. Then I introduce these cases by saying, "Here are three companies that took actions that either helped other people (Johnson & Johnson and Merck) or that preserved the environment (Herman Miller). Those actions were expensive. The companies are large and can afford the expense, but there were certainly other uses for the money: increased dividends, higher wages, more R&D. Was it "right" to take these actions? If you feel these actions were "right", then how would you convince members of the financial community – brokerage firms and investment banks – who did tentatively object? If you feel they were "wring", then how would you convince members of their boards of directors who did strongly approve?

I then divide each of the sections of the class (right, center and left) into small three to four person groups, and give them 20 minutes to decide "yes, take the action" or "no, don't take the action" for "their" case, and write out their decision and their supporting rationale on a vue graph transparency. After 20 minutes the class reassembles, and I call upon one group from each section to present their report.

The reports inevitably approve the expenditures for social or environmental purposes. A cynic could claim that it is not their money that the students are spending so casually for the benefit of people other than the stockholders. But, members of my classes apparently truly do believe that actions of this nature do build pride in the company and cohesion among the workforce, and also bring a spirit of excitement and adventure to the firm. Towards the end of the class I put on the vue-graph slides of the stock performance of each of the three firms over time. Their price performance histories are very impressive.

Johnson and Johnson and the Recall of Tylenol

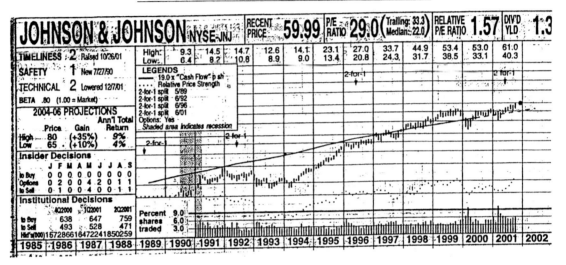

I suggest that you spend some time talking about the Mission Statement or "Credo" of Johnson and Johnson. A copy in large type, suitable for display on an overhead projector or vue-graph, is on the next page. It lists the major duties of the firm, in order of priority, as 1) customers, 2) employees, 3) communities, and 4) owners. My students never seem to find that sequence all that unusual, and I have to remind them of the usual placement of the owners at the top. My students particularly like the statements about the dignity, worth, security and opportunity for the employees.

Herman Miller and Preservation of the Environment

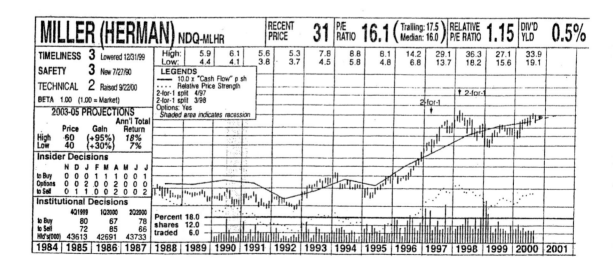

Mission Statement of Johnson and Johnson

We believe that our first responsibility is for the doctors, nurses, and patients, to mothers and all others who use our products and services.

- In meeting their needs everything we do must be of high quality
- We must constantly strive to reduce our costs in order to maintain reasonable prices
- Customer orders must be serviced promptly and accurately
- Our suppliers and distributors must have an opportunity to make a fair profit.

We are responsible to our employees, the men and women who work with us throughout the world.

- Everyone must be considered as an individual. We must respect their dignity and recognize their worth
- They must have a sense of security in their jobs. Compensation must be fair and adequate and working conditions clean, orderly and safe.
- Employees must feel free to make suggestions and complaints
- There must be equal treatment for employment, development and advancement for those qualified
- We must provide competent management and their actions must be just and ethical

We are responsible to the communities in which we live and work, and to the world community as well.

- We must be good citizens – support good works and charities and bear our fair share of taxes
- We must encourage civic improvements and better health and education
- We must maintain in good order the proper ty we are privileged to use, protecting the environment and natural resources

Our final responsibility is to our stockholders. Business must make a sound profit

- We must experiment with new ideas. Research must be carried on, innovative programs developed, and mistakes paid for.
- New equipment must be purchased, new facilities provided, and new products launched
- Reserves must be created to provide for adverse times
- When we operate according to these principles, the stockholders should realize a fair return.

Merck Corporation and the Cure for River Blindness

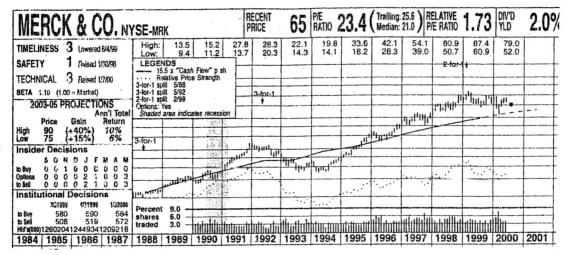

At the end of the class I explain that there are other companies that have taken generous actions to help others, or to preserve the environment, that have not succeeded, that generosity is not a certain pathway to success. It does, however, build pride in the company and reliance upon the willingness of management to go beyond normal economic outcomes. I put the graphic that dominates Chapter V on the vue graph (reproduced in large type on the following page), and make the following four points:

1. Companies cannot – in the exceedingly competitive conditions of the modern economy – succeed without cooperation, innovation and unification among all of the participants in the typical extended firm: employees at all levels, suppliers, distributors, customers, communities, and owners. Those are exactly the groups mentioned in Johnson and Johnson's Credo, or Mission Statement.

2. Companies also cannot, once more in the exceedingly competitive conditions of the modern economy —achieve cooperation, innovation and unification among all of the participants in the typical extended firm without trust, commitment and effort. Trust is the key. Trust in the future intentions, actions and policies of management. If the participants have no trust, why should they make the needed commitment and effort?

3. Managers cannot build that trust in their future intentions, actions and policies unless they adopt a philosophy of management that combines economic outcomes, legal requirements and ethical duties. Neither one by itself is enough, but jointly they provide a means to convincingly explain the fairness of decisions. All participants in the firm cannot have everything they want. There has to be a balance that is perceived as "fair".

4. The establishment of a balance that is perceived as "fair" is the function of management. That balance then has to be expressed in the organizational values, corporate goals and mission statement, and then implemented by financial supports, performance measures, incentive payments, prohibited procedures and leadership actions. That expression, and that implementation, I conclude, will be the topic of Chapter VI.

Cooperation, Innovation and Unification

Managerial
balancing:
-Economic benefits
-Legal requirements
-Ethical Principles

Organizational
Values

Corporate
Goals

Mission
Statement

Financial
Supports

Performance
Measures

Incentive
Payments

Prohibited
Procedures

Leadership
Actions

Trust
Commitment ⟶ Innovation
Effort

Cooperation
Innovation
Unification

Teaching Notes for Chapter VI – How Can a Business Organization Be Made Moral?

The basic message of this chapter is that it is not enough for the senior executives in a company to balance economic outcomes, legal requirements and ethical duties in their decisions and actions. They must also infuse that changed philosophy of management throughout the firm by clearly combing organizational values and corporate goals into an explicit mission statement, and then implementing that mission statement with financial supports, performance measures, incentive payments, prohibited procedures and leadership actions. This, of course, was the conclusion of Chapter V, and was summarized in the following graphic:

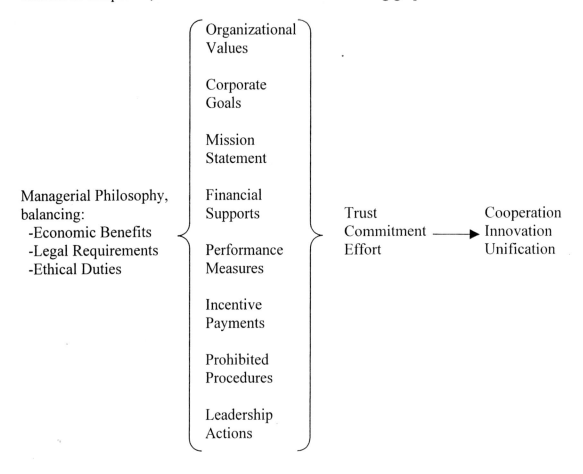

Chapter VI used the example of the wreck of the Exxon Valdez as an example of the need to infuse a changed philosophy of management throughout the firm. The argument can easily be made that Exxon's senior executives focused only upon economic outcomes and neglected legal requirements and ethical duties as they formed a cost competitive strategy in response to continual reductions in the global price of crude oil. The result was a lack of breadth of purpose, a shortage of equipment, an absence of training, and an eventual absolute disaster to the Alaskan environment and the company's reputation. :

I generally use the Wreck of the Exxon Valdez as if it were a case to structure the discussion on the day I assign Chapter VI, but with very specific assignment questions to different groups of students. By this stage of the course I feel that I can ask students to meet in groups before class, and come prepared to explain a portion of the case to the balance of the class. Here are the assignment questions I use; they are based upon the graphic that describes the causes and consequences of the wreck and slow clean-up contained in the text.

1. The tanker Exxon Valdez was wrecked on what has been termed "the clearest marked reef in Prince William Sound", with the following immediate causes. Why did this happen? Why was there this obvious lack of commitment and effort?:

Improper behavior
of the ship's captain

Improper position of
the ship's lookout

Improper change of
the ship's course

               Wreck of the tanker
               on clearest marked

Improper use of   reef in PW Sound
ship's auto-pilot

Unlicensed and in-
experienced 3rd mate

Overworked and
tired ship's crew

2. Following the wreck of the tanker the Alyeska terminal (partially owned by Exxon) was unable to respond promptly or effectively, despite the existence of a contract with the state of Alaska specifying the terms of that response. Why did this happen?

Shortages of on-site
equipment
 -recovery barges
 -recovery booms
 -repair parts
 -pumps & hoses

               Unable to contain &
Shortages of on-site   recover oil following
personnel   agreed-upon plan
 -lack of skills
 -lack of training
 -lack of cohesion

Disbanded oil spill
& refinery fire teams

3. Was Lawrence Rawl responsible? At the annual meeting of the Exxon Corporation, held in May, 1990 (two months after the disaster in Prince William Sound) a group of protestors called for the resignation of Mr. Lawrence Rawl, Chairman of the Board of Exxon. One protestor who was also a stockholder took the microphone during the question and answer period at the end of that meeting and asked Mr. Rawl, "Will you resign, and if not, why not?" What is your feeling; should Lawrence Rawl resign? Was he responsible for the wreck and slow clean up?

4. For the next six questions assume that the members of your group were senior members of a corporate level consulting firm approached by Lawrence Rawl before the wreck occurred . Assume that Lawrence Rawl was a very different sort of manager than the "profits only" person he appears to be in the case. Assume that he told the members of your group that he was worried that as a result of the constant chopping and cutting employees at all levels and regions of Exxon was becoming inattentive to the possibility of a severe environmental disaster. He asked members of your consulting firm to address the following issues:

a) How should the philosophy of management of the company be changed. Assume that Lawrence Rawl admitted that it was now far too oriented towards economic outcomes only. What else, he asked, should be included.

b) What should be the organizational values, the corporate goals and the mission statement of Exxon Corp? Assume that he said that Exxon had to broaden it's duties and goals, and express those clearly in a mission statement for all employees to read and understand

c) What should be the financial supports? That is, how should the capital allocation and cost budgeting procedures be changed. Assume he said that was certainly a need to reduce investments and cut costs, but not at the expense of basic safety?

d) What should be the performance measures? How should his performance as Chairman of Exxon be measured? How should the performance of the manager of the Alyeska terminal be measured? Suggest a few incentive payments also to reinforce those measures.

e) What should be some prohibited procedures? List five to ten procedures or actions or conditions that simply would not be tolerated by the company and that, had they been in effect prior to the accident, would have greatly reduced its probability and/or severity.

f) What should be some leadership actions? List two to three dramatic actions, or memorable statements, that Lawrence Rawl might make that would convey to all members of the company the importance of protecting the environment and avoiding accidents.

I would suggest that you start the class by showing a videotape. Videos are always popular with students, and in this instance the recommended video is very relevant to the topic: *The Wreck of the Exxon Valdez*. This is a 40 minute tape, available from Alaskan Video Productions in Anchorage. Forty minutes is too long; I would suggest that you pick out sections that you want to show, and then fast forward between those sections, so that you have plenty of time for discussion at the end. The tape describes the sequence of events that led to the accident;

Sequence of Events in the Wreck of the Exxon Valdez

Improper behavior
of the ship's captain

Improper position of
the ship's lookout

Improper change of
the ship's course

Improper use of
ship's auto-pilot

Unlicensed and in-
experienced 3rd mate

Overworked and
tired ship's crew

Shortages of on-site
equipment
 -recovery barges
 -recovery booms
 -repair parts
 -pumps & hoses

Shortages of on-site
personnel
 -lack of skills
 -lack of training
 -lack of cohesion

Disbanded oil spill
& refinery fire teams

Wreck of the tanker
on clearest marked
reef in PW Sound

Unable to contain &
recover oil following
agreed-upon plan

Large oil spill was
not contained and
coated 750 miles
of Alaska coastline

Destroyed catch sources
of commercial fishers

Destroyed food sources
of native peoples

Killed 40% of bald
eagles in Alaska

Killed 80% of sea
otters in PW Sound

Killed 300,000 (est)
sea & shore birds

Resulted in $2.3 billion
gov't fine against Exxon

Resulted in $3.4 billion
legal award against Exxon

shows the results in the damaged shoreline and the dying seabirds and sea otters, and ends with the confrontation between a protester and Mr. Rawls at the annual meeting of the Exxon Corporation that was described in the third assignment question: "Will you resign, and if not, why not?"

That apparently would make a perfect place to start the class discussion, but I suggest that you delay getting to that issue. Firstly make certain that everyone understands the reasons for the total lack of commitment and effort on the ship and the total lack of preparation on the shore. Here are the issues that I think ought to be covered in response to the full set of assignment questions:

1. What were the causes of the wreck of the Exxon Valdez; why did it run aground on the "clearest marked reef in Prince William Sound"?

2. What were the causes of the slow response by Alyeska Terminal, why were they unable to perform as promised in the contract with the state of Alaska. The two are similar, and will be covered jointly:

    External causes (world events) were 1) the falling crude oil prices which meant that the oil Exxon produced from their own wells was worth far less on the world market; 2) the increasing technology which made possible automated tankers and smaller crews; and 3) the lack of accidents for 18 years which results in a feeling of overconfidence.

    Corporate causes (senior executives) were the continual cost cutting. Rawl seemed to feel that reducing costs was his only job; he certainly never mentions in the various quotations any recognition of a need to consider morale or safety. 40,000 employees out of 145 were forced to retire, and the oil spill response and refine fire teams were disbanded

    Divisional causes (middle level mangers) were acceptance of the directive to cut costs and lower investments. Doubtless their performance was measured on cost control and investment reduction, and rewarded when they succeeded. They forced others to cut corners and take chances in order to "make the numbers"

    Operational causes (lower level managers, on the tanker or at the terminal). Cutting corners to "make the numbers" resulted in the tanker with unlicensed 3rd mate and overworked, tired crew. The oil terminal lacked barges, booms, repair parts, pumps, hoses and dispersants, and had workers who lacked skills and training.

    Attitudinal causes (employees throughout the company). No one seemed to care. Certainly no one reported the capital for drinking. The ship lookout was not at station. The barge was not repaired. The inventory was not checked. The training was not performed. In a telling illustration, a hose was not unrolled.

3. Was Lawrence Rawl responsible? Should he resign? One argument is that Lawrence was at corporate headquarters at the time of the accident, not Prince William Sound, and that the chairman of a company the size of Exxon cannot be expected to personally examine tanker

captains for intoxication at every sailing, nor personally verify the inventory of emergency supplies at every terminal. This argument would continue that Lawrence Rawl had delegated responsibility for the staffing of the tankers and the maintenance of the supplies to other executives; if any executives should resign, it should be those people. The other argument, however, is that Rawl created the conditions that led to problems in the staffing of tankers and the maintenance of supplies. Here you can spend some time on the meaning of the term "responsibity". Is a manager responsible only for the activities he/she directly oversees, or is he/she responsible for the conditions that mould those activities? If he/she accepts credit for the successes that come from those conditions, then should he/she accept blame for the failures? As you doubtless can tell, I strongly believe in the latter. My belief is that Lawrence Rawl should have resigned.

4. How should the philosophy of management at Exxon be changed? At the time of the wreck it focused only on economic outcomes, and did not truly recognize legal requirements (acts on the tanker were in conflict with Coast Guard regulations and conditions at the terminal were in conflict with Alaskan laws) nor ethical duties.

Harms were being imposed on the local fishermen, with increased risk to their livelihood, and on state residents, with increased risk to their environment.

Rights were being denied to state citizens who certainly have a right to have shipping rules and spill contracts obeyed, and to fishermen who have a right to pursue livelihood

Ethical duties about openness, honesty and pride were being ignored, as were universal duties. Senior executives would not have wanted these conditions near their homes.

5. What should have been organizational values, corporate goals and the mission statement? Exxon is the largest company in the petroleum industry; perhaps they should have led by example:

Corporate values. What does the company owe different groups?
- Customers – excellent service and quality products at competitive prices
- Employees – excellent training, decent conditions and opportunities for advancement
- Suppliers/distributors – full information and opportunities for growth and participation
- Local residents – absolute protection against oil spills & fires
- State citizens – absolute adherence to the law
- Owners – profits after obligations to others (as in Johnson & Johnson Credo)

Organizational goals. What does the company want to achieve?
- Industry position – be #1
- Process efficiency – be the leader
- Technical capability – be the leader
- Employee loyalty – be the leader
- Environmental protection – be the leader

Mission statement. We will be the dominant company in the global oil industry. We will achieve that position by providing excellent service and quality products at competitive prices. That n turn will require advanced technical capability and outstanding process efficiency. That, again in turn, will require dedicated managers, engineers and workers who are trained in our methods and proud of our operations. We will provide that training and build that pride by being the absolute best in all of the areas of our responsibility and in all of the divisions of our firm.

6. Financial supports. How should the capital allocation and cost budgeting procedures be changed? How can the company achieve economic efficiency and yet not reduce investments and cut costs at the expense of basic safety?

    Capital allocations. Equipment and supplies to contain and recover oil spills were rejected in the past because they did not meet roi targets. Company should include costs of large environmental disasters (clean-up fees, government fines and civil suits) in their estimates of cash flow

    Cost budgets. Company needed more people on the tankers and more training for their shore personnel. Those were rejected in the past by insistence upon predetermined budgets that ignored needs. Budgets should meet needs and goals, as shown in the mission statement

7. Performance measures. How should the performance of the chairman (Lawrence Rawl) and of the manager of the Alyeska oil terminal be measured? Currently they seem to be measured only on profits, revenues and/or costs.

    Chairman (or all employees at headquarters)
    - Industry position – relative to other firms
    - Technical capability (all divisions) – annual new products/processes
    - Process efficiency (all processes) – measured by benchmarked costs
    - Customer satisfaction (all markets) – measured by surveys
    - Employee loyalty (all divisions) – measured by turnover and surveys
    - Environmental protection (all locations) – measured by readiness to respond with trained crew and needed supplies
    - Legal adherence (all locations) – measured by number of claims and number of situations with the potential to create claims.
    - Financial performance (corporate) – measured by ros (profits/sales) and roi (profits/investment)

    Manger at oil terminal (or all employees at the terminal)
    - Technical capability (local) – annual new products/processes
    - Process efficiency (local) – measured by benchmarked costs
    - Customer satisfaction (local, if relevant) – measured by surveys
    - Employee loyalty (local) – measured by turnover and surveys
    - Environmental protection (local) – measured by readiness to respond with trained crew and needed supplies

- Legal adherence (local) – measured by number of claims and number of situations with the potential to create claims.
- Financial performance (local) – measured by ros (profits/sales) and roi (profits/investment)

8. Prohibited practices. The instructions were to list five to ten procedures or actions or behaviors that simply would not be tolerated by the firm. Generally these are listed in strong negative terms:
   - Never be intoxicated when at work
   - Never fail to be at proper position on shipboard
   - Never ignore Coast Guard regulations
   - Never fail to have emergency equipment/supplies on hand
   - Never cut costs at the expense of employee or environmental safety
   - Never conduct lackadaisical training exercises

9. Leadership actions. What could Rawl have done, or said, that would create an impression and convey the importance he should have put upon workplace and environmental safety
   - Hold unannounced exercises to ensure that training and suppliers are proper
   - Conduct personal visits to ensure that training and supplies are proper
   - Announce that, in the event of an accident, all senior level executives will be required to participate in the clean-up
   - Continually emphasize the values, goals and mission of the company
   - "We at Exxon will be #1 in oil and #1 in safety"

Two Companies in Need of Redesign (Sarah Goodwin)

These are two companies in which recent graduates of a business school (Sarah Goodwin at a department store and Susan Shapiro at a chemical company) were forced to face "where do I draw the line" moral problems soon after graduation. The analysis of the moral content of those cases was described in the sections of this teaching guide following Chapters II and III. I will not repeat that moral analysis here. Instead, the assignment for the students now is that they are to take the place of a senior executive within those firms who has just found that the practice described in the case is not an anomaly but is prevalent throughout the company. What should they do? Specifically, what should a senior executive at the department store that had hired, and then fired, Sarah Goodwin do to ensure that the described sort of action (shipping infested food products to convenience stores in a very poor section of the city) never happens again.

Probably a good place to start is to understand the sequence of causes. High end departments stores, such as Saks 5th Avenue, Nieman Marcus, Lord & Taylor, no longer hold a dominant position in fashion retailing. Small specialty shops and original designer sales through mass merchants have provided substantial competition, and the old down-town locations of many of the "flag ship" department stores no longer attracted style-centered customers. Senior executives at the "high end" stores did not reposition their companies, except for building branch locations in suburban malls. Instead they placed increased pressure on their buyers to find style copies quickly from Asia, reduce inventories, cut costs and meet "stretch" or challenging budgets. Most buyers were measured and rewarded on a profits per square foot basis. The buyers found that they were losing their prestige and authority. Many just gave up; decided to do what was needed to get by until retirement. They took chances and cut corners. They no longer worried about what might happen to the department store. Profits now seemed to be the only thing that mattered; not reputation or style. If enough pressures on put on obtaining profits by senior level executives, mid-level managers will oblige with profits and risks.

The following are some very specific suggestions for possible changes, following the what-I-hope-is-now-familiar graphic that was part of the assignment. These are difficult for me to express for the department store; I know nothing about "high end" department store retailing, but I assume price is less important than style, and that the desire is to dominate the style conscious market segment within a sophisticated urban population:

1. Organizational values. Organizational values are the duties the firm owes to the individuals, groups and organizations associated with the success of the firm
   - Customers –high style, good quality, adequate price and <u>excellent</u> service
   - Buyers – continual opportunities to demonstrate style selection and supplier relationship skills
   - Suppliers – continual treatment as an integral part of the company, with full information on style choices and sales trends
   - Owners – if we can tie together customers, buyers and suppliers, profits will follow

2. Corporate goals. Corporate goals are the end points the firm wants to achieve on various dimensions of success
   - Industry position – we want to dominate the high style, good quality, adequate price and excellent service segment of our industry.
   - Market share. We expect to have over 50% of the market share for this segment of the retailing industry
   - Technological achievement – we will have the most advanced information system in this segment of the retailing industry
   - Buyer competence – we will have the most competent buyers, adept at judging clothing style and maintaining supplier relationships, within this segment of the industry
   - Supplier loyalty – we will have the most dedicated suppliers within our segment of the retailing industry

3. Mission statement. Our company will dominate the high style, good quality, adequate price and unsurpassed service industry. We will accomplish this by combining buyer opportunity, information technology and supplier trust. To achieve the needed level of cooperation and trust we will treat everyone associated with our firm with dignity and respect.

4. Financial supports. We will clearly need a substantial capital investment in information technology, both hardware and software. We assume that this investment will meet roi targets, so no special analysis is needed to justify the expenditure.

5. Performance evaluations. Performance evaluations are the measures of what a person, a group or a division is doing to observe the duties and achieve the goals of the mission statement.

Measures of performance for the president of the department store chain:
- Quality and usefulness of the information base
- Share of the selected market segment
- Style "hits' by the buyers
- Customer satisfaction (national), from repeat customers and surveys
- Employee satisfaction (national), from turnover and surveys
- Suppliers satisfaction (all), from personal visits and surveys
- Annual growth/decline in sales (national)
- Annual growth/decline in profits (national)

Measures of performance for the buyers in the department store chains
- Service quality, from secret shoppers
- Style "hit" selection, from sales revenue response
- Customer satisfaction (local), from repeat customers and surveys
- Employee satisfaction (local), from turnover and surveys
- Suppliers satisfaction (departmental), from personal visits and surveys
- Annual growth/decline in sales (local)
- Annual growth/decline in profits (local)

6. Incentive payments. Incentive payments are usually tied to the performance evaluations; they are to reward those who perform well. They might include:
- an award of $10,000 for the store employee who provides the best customer service of the quarter as judged by a secret shopper
- a bonus of $5,000 for the buyer with the best repeat customer ratio for the quarter
- a bonus of $5,000 for the buyer with the best supplier satisfaction index for the quarter. .

7. Prohibited procedures. Prohibited procedures are those activities or behaviors that are never to be undertaken for they will result in immediate discharge:
- Never lie to or mislead suppliers
- Never lie to or mislead employees
- Never harm non-customers or local residents

8. Leadership actions. Leadership actions are the personal relationships and memorable statements of the president:
- Maintain open door policy
- Frequent store visits
- Frequent supplier visits
- Continual duty/goal/mission reiteration.

Two Companies in Need of Redesign (Susan Shapiro)

In this instance employees were being exposed to benzene, a known carcinogen that also causes birth defects, though the chemical process exposing the workers was technically legal because it was "open air," located in a shed without walls. The vapor accumulated on still days, with no wind, in levels that far exceeded the federal standard. Capital requests to improve the situation have been rejected, according to the plant manager, because they did not meet targeted rates of return and "insisting upon funding for a project that won't meet targeted rates of return is a sure-fire way around here to be shown the door marked exit in large black letters."

The assignment for the students in this iteration of the Susan Shapiro case is to assume that they are a senior executive within the chemical company who has just found that the practice described in the case (blatant disregard of workplace safety) is not an anomaly but is prevalent throughout the company. What should he/she do?

Probably a good place to start is to understand the sequence of causes. The "basic" petrochemical industry (companies who produce standard chemical products, such as plastic or fertilizers, in bulk, for very large customers) has become very competitive. The process technologies have become widely known, the raw materials have become easily available, and the needed capital has become easily raised. Companies operating in 2nd or ever 3rd world nations have a number of distinct cost advantages: worker wages, safety regulations and environmental requirements are all much lower overseas. Senior executives in the domestic basic or commodity chemical companies in many instances did not invest in new products or processes (both very "iffy" for the basic products such as plastics and fertilizers); instead they tried to drive down costs and lower capital investments. As in the case of Exxon, the operating managers took chances and cut corners attempting to reach these new targets, and the result – in the plant visited by Susan Shapiro soon after she started work for the firm – was a very unsafe though fully legal benzine "washing" process to remove surface impurities from one of the commodity products.

The following are some very specific suggestions for possible changes in values, goals, mission, etc. I assume in this instance that, if this company is to compete in the global economy, it will be necessary to invest substantially in advanced process automation and bring costs down and product and service quality up through technology.

1. Organizational values. Organizational values are the duties the firm owes to the individuals, groups and organizations associated with the success of the firm
   - Customers –high quality products and on-time delivery from automated processes
   - Workers – continual training for the skilled, not manual. jobs in automated processes
   - Engineers – money and people needed to continually develop new automated processes
   - Managers – money and people needed to continually install new automated processes
   - Owners – if we can develop, finance and operate new processes, profits will follow

2. Corporate goals. Corporate goals are the end points the firm wants to achieve on various dimensions of success
   - Technological capability – be the leader
   - Process innovation – be the leader
   - Manufacturing efficiency – be #1
   - Customer satisfaction – aim for 100%
   - Workplace safety – aim for 100%
   - Environmental protection – aim for 100%

3. Mission statement. Our company will be #1 in manufacturing efficiency in the basic chemical industry for commodity plastics and fertilizers. That position will enable us to provide our customers with excellent product quality, on-time delivery, and competitive prices. We will achieve this position by investing the capital and spending the money necessary to be a leader in technological capability, process innovation and employee capability. This change will require a substantial commitment and definite effort by everyone associated with the firm; that commitment and effort will be recognized with fairness and justice by the stockholders and managers.

4. Financial supports. It is an assumption that such a "manufacturing efficiency" strategy would be viable in the basic chemical industry. Accepting that assumption, how should such a strategy be implemented in a way that pulls the full firm together and leaves no one out. Clearly the company will need increased capital investment in better laboratory facilities and improved process equipment. That should meet roi targets. Clearly also the company will need increased capital investment in workplace safety; that will be justified by meeting the stated goals of the firm.

5. Performance evaluations. Performance evaluation are the measures of what a person, a group or a division is doing to observe the duties and achieve the goals of the mission statement. I would suggest that these be more oriented towards operations than towards profits:

    Performance evaluations for the president of the chemical company:
    - Benchmarked cost of chemical process
    - Annual installation of improved processes
    - Annual development of improved processes
    - Annual training of process workers
    - Customer satisfaction
    - Worker loyalty
    - Public perception

    Performance evaluations for a plant manager for the chemical company
    - Benchmarked cost of chemical process
    - Annual installation of improved processes
    - Annual development of improved processes
    - Annual training of process workers
    - Customer satisfaction
    - Worker loyalty and retention
    - Workplace safety
    - Environmental protection

6. Incentive payments. Incentive payments are rewards for meeting the targets set by the performance evaluation measures. I would suggest that these combine money and recognition, and be oriented towards the plant managers (assuming that there are multiple plants) who lead in the various categories of the performance evaluation:

Incentive payments for plant managers
- $50,000 bonus for plant manager who leads in manufacturing efficiency
- $25,000 bonus for plant manager who leads in customer satisfaction
- $25,000 bonus for plant manager who leads in worker loyalty & retention

7. Prohibited procedures. Prohibited procedures are those decisions or action that are never to be undertaken for they will result in immediate discharge:
- Never continue unsafe workplace conditions; fix or close the operation
- Never ignore accidental discharges; fix or close the operation

8. Leadership actions. Leadership actions are the personal relationships and memorable words of the president and other senior executive officers
- Open door policy
- Frequent plant and district visits
- Continual duty/goal/mission reiteration
- Continual emphasis on being #1 in manufacturing efficiency

McKinstrey Advertising Company

I am not going to do the teaching notes for the last two cases in this section of the book in such agonizing detail. I assume that it is clear how to follow the graphic outline that relates organizational values, corporate goals, the mission statement, financial supports, performance measures, incentive payments, prohibited procedures and leadership actions if you wish to do so in your classes. Instead, I will just describe much more briefly how I handle the discussions in my own classes.

I like the McKinstrey Advertising Agency case. It is much more complex than it seems on the surface, and I often use it to end the course. A client of the agency has developed a new radar and laser detector for automobiles that will enable drivers to speed without fear of detection by the police. The client wants McKinstrey to prepare the advertising to commercialize the product. One of the associates in the agency, Marilynn Schaefer, refuses to work on the account; she feels that it is not "right" to market radar and laser detectors that lead to higher vehicle speeds and consequently to more highway accidents and greater human injury, suffering and deaths. Unfortunately for McKinstrey the client has specifically asked that Marilynn be assigned to the account – they were very pleased with her work on an earlier product – and when she continued to refuse that assignment the account executive fires her, saying "Either work on this account for me or don't work at this agency for anyone".

The assignment question places the student in the position of the president of the agency. Marilynn has come to him/her and said that she should not be fired for following her conscience. George, when contacted, refuses to budge, saying that employees don't have the right to pick and choose the work that they will or won't do. There are two ways to handle the resolution of these issues in class. One is the standard case discussion format; the other consists of prepared group reports. I will describe both in this teaching note.

For the standard case discussion I start the class by asking, "What should the president do?" and I'm always disappointed to find that the first few students simply jump into the interpersonal dispute between Marilynn and George as if it were a "people problem", and recommend "sitting down" with either one or both in an attempt to negotiate a compromise. This may go on for some time, and occasionally I have to intervene, but usually some member of the class will say "Wait a minute, I think that Marilynn does have a point in her refusal to market the detector".

Then we get into whether it is "right" or "wrong" to sell radar and laser speed detectors. The arguments, in brief, are 1) economic benefits – there is a market for the product and customer are informed, but the law is certainly questionable and the external costs are very real; 2) legal requirements – there is no law against selling the detectors, due to the Interstate Commerce clause in the Constitution, but there is a law against using them in many states, so those laws conflict; and 3) ethical duties -- the actions of the company in selling the detector are certainly open in that they plan to advertise it, but the sale will not bring everyone – police, drivers and potential victims – together in pursuit of a common goal, and there probably is not a net social benefit in the time saved for speeders versus the injuries caused by speeding.

The class usually divides, with one third saying that it is permissible to sell the detectors, and two thirds saying that it is "wrong". I then stop the class, and tell students that it probably would not be possible to verbally talk George into the "it's wrong" camp, or Marilynn into the "it's permissible" sector in that their positions are too set by their ongoing dispute. Instead, I organize small discussion groups (4 to 5 persons) from each of those camps or sectors, and ask them to prepare a list of values and goals for McKinstrey Advertising, and then combine those goals and values into a mission statement. Maybe, I explain, the mission statement will emphasize enough common ground that the two individuals will see their differences in a new light and both will stay. If not, at least the values, goals and mission of the company will be clear, and this sort of problem will be avoided in the future.

The students groups are told to put their goals, values and final mission statement on a vue graph transparency, and given twenty minutes to prepare that transparency. Because this will be the third class on this topic twenty minutes seems to be enough. Three or four of those groups are asked to explain their proposals. We talk a little about how to carry those statements forward with performance measures and incentive payments, etc. and then take a vote on 1) will this new definition of the organization will help to avoid these sorts of disputes in the future (the vote in inevitably favorable) and 2) whether this new definition of the organization will help to convince the two protagonists to stay (generally but not overwhelmingly favorable). I generally – as shown in "Suggested Schedule for a 14-Class Module on Business Ethics" in the first section of this teaching note – have this as the last class. I summarize what I hope students have learned from the module, say "thank you", and quit.

The prepared group report approach, i think, provides a more certain way to end the course. By this time in the semester members of the class know each other reasonably well so I ask them to form groups of three to four students. Then I divide those groups into four different-segments, with a specific assignment for each one:

- Groups in the 1st segment are to decide if the action – promoting the use of a new type of radar speed detector – is "right" or "wrong", and to prepare a report on vue-graph slides or Power Point.
- Groups in the 2nd segment are to assume that the senior executives have decided that promoting speed detectors is "right" and they prepare a report on values, goals, a mission statement, etc. based upon that assumption.
- Groups in the 3rd segment are to assume that the senior executive have decided that promoting speed detectors is "wrong" and they are to state values and goals, prepare a mission statement, etc. based upon that assumption.
- Groups in the 4th segment have no assignment; instead they are to play the role of members of the board of directors of the advertising agency, or members of the senior partnership council. The listen to the reports from the other groups, and then vote on what is to be done.
- Instead of giving the groups time during the class to prepare their reports, I generally insist that the groups meet prior to class and come in with their reports prepared and ready for presentation. It is a good way to end the course.

Boston Company and Firing the Chairman

This is a good case to define the responsibilities of the senior executives of a business firm, though I seldom use it. The issues are the same as have already been covered in the Wreck of the Exxon Valdez. Are senior managers responsible just for making profits and obeying laws, or are they responsible for creating an organization that will do both over time? In short, are they responsible for creating an organization that will adhere to stated values and achieve stated goals in a way that will avoid the "cutting corners" and "taking chances" that seem so often to come from intense pressure for financial performance. These are the issue involved with Enron, a corporate bankruptcy that is much in the news as I write these notes

Boston Company, as described in the case, was an old New England bank and trust company that had become stodgy, with little growth and low profits. It was purchased by a Wall Street investment bank, and the new owners brought in an active new chairman to shake things up: William von Germeten. He quickly made a number of changes in pursuit of that "shake things up" goal:

- Market focus changed from an established wealthy elite to a younger more modern customer base, who often enjoyed a celebrity status
- Company personnel changed from older, conservative employees who did have an admirable investment record to more aggressive recent graduates, often trained in quantitative finance
- High performance targets were set for growth in assets, loans, stock and bond funds, revenues and profits.
- Large cash incentives were established for managers who met those growth oriented goals; they could double their salaries, and earn up to $1 million per year.
- Luxurious "perks" were also offered to the managers who met their goals; they were invited to lavish parties, given expensive automobiles
- All these changes created immense pressures to perform. Von Germeten said he found nothing wrong with that. He explained that he was under pressure to perform as well.

There is no question but that von Germeten drove the Boston Company hard to increase profits, to become part of the investment banking culture. There were the financial successes he could claim:

- Deposits increased 18 times
- Mortgages and loans increased 10 times
- Private trust funds increased 8 times
- Public trust funds increased 6 times
- Profits increased 12 times (from $12 million/yr to $150 million/yr)

There is also no question but that a lot of things went wrong towards the end of von Germeten's nine year tenure. These are the financial problems he should recognize, though he claimed that he was not responsible

- Comptroller refused to approve the accounting records; said that revenues were being recognized before they occurred, and expenses were being recorded after they became due
- Manager of internal trust fund committed suicide; public audit following his death showed a unrecorded loss of $10 million on a $100 million investment in unsuitable securities
- Outside auditors found an additional $10 to $15 million loss in "accounting irregularities", a figure that later grew to $30 to $45 million.
- Jumbo loan portfolio had to write off $90 million in uncollectable loans $15 million loss, and then an additional $30 million loss

The final totals were an increased in profits of $450 million over three years, and a series of losses of $195 million in a single year. Von Germeten insisted that he had done nothing wrong, that he had changed the focus of the company, and brought in new people and instilled new targets, measures and incentives to get much better results. He was not responsible, he continued, for the fact that some people had cheated to meet the targets and receive the incentives. Von Germeten did not make this claim, but he could – as has been done in the instance of one or two people at Enron – have stated that the fault lay with the Business Schools for not adequately training their graduates in ethics.

When I do use this case in class I try to achieve acceptance among the students that management goes far beyond just selecting targets, setting goals, demanding results and providing rewards. They have all heard approving stories about "tough" corporate level managers who have combined continually increasing standards with threats of discharge and incentives of money to create a performance ethos. I want them to come to understand that if you put enough pressure on people they will find ways of meeting short term goals that are counterproductive over the long-term. Maybe management is not just generating profits. Maybe management is building companies that operate with a sense of trust, commitment and effort to achieve success on a number of dimensions over lengthy time periods. That is what I think the ethics of management is all about: achieving cooperation, innovation and unification within extended organizations during periods of global competition and continual change.